Other books by Al Clark

Raymond Chandler in Hollywood
Making Priscilla
The Lavender Bus

Time Flies

Al Clark

Brandl & Schlesinger

First published in Australia by Brandl & Schlesinger in 2021.

www.brandl.com.au

Hardcover edition published in collaboration with Literati, Inc. in 2022 in the United States and Canada.

Cover and book design by Andras Berkes-Brandl

Cover photograph: Al Clark, Los Angeles 1979, © Pennie Smith

ISBN 978-0-6485233-7-6 (paperback)

ISBN 978-1-7374508-1-8 (hardcover)

ISBN 978-0-6485233-8-3 (epdf)

ISBN 978-0-6485233-9-0 (epub)

A catalogue record for this book is available from the

National Library of Australia.

Printed in the United States by McNaughton & Gunn on Forest Stewardship Council® certified paper.

for Lesley, Jason and Louise
and for Andrena, Rachel and Jamie

ACKNOWLEDGEMENTS

As my immersion in filmmaking escalated during the second half of my life, so the impact of the first half – the compound of experiences that had brought me to that point – became correspondingly more vivid.

I decided to write an account of those times, increasingly aware as I did so of the people, and the memories, that fuelled them.

I thank in particular all my family, a stable constant in a fragmented life; my earliest employers – Tony Elliott and Richard Branson, to whom I owe the many opportunities their confidence in me provided; my friends and colleagues along the way; and Richard Burridge, whose enthusiasm and sound advice during the book's home stretch accelerated me towards the finishing line.

An appreciative *gracias* to both Brandl and Schlesinger.

And a loving salute to the Cinema Corrales – still standing – without which there would be nothing else.

CHAPTER ONE

The cans began their odyssey in Seville.

It was there that the film distribution companies based in Madrid and Barcelona had established regional offices from which to circulate prints of their movies to the towns and villages of Andalucia, the southernmost area of Spain, the one closest – in location, topography, architecture, heritage and spirit – to North Africa.

These cans, containing the reels of film, were placed in a hessian sack and loaded into the luggage compartment of a passenger bus, which travelled 92 kilometres to the southwest along a winding single-lane highway punctuated by a dozen villages, to Huelva, a shipping port halfway to the Portuguese border, on the banks of the deep, tidal, treacherous River Odiel.

The sack was collected at the terminal by Alonso, an electrician who had taken the morning off work to do this because his boss, the head of the electrical department in the mining village across the river, was also the manager of its cinema. Alonso carried the sack on his shoulder through the town across roads, through gardens, past fountains, down to the pier, where he waited to board the small motorboat that ferried passengers to the opposite bank and beyond. Then, disembarking at a creaky wooden jetty in the marshes, he secured the sack to the back of the bicycle he had left there earlier in the day, and rode slowly along the dirt track next to the railway line that led to Corrales, a whitewashed mirage suspended in the leaden stillness of the midday sun.

His final destination was the village cinema, to which he had his own key. Inside the lobby, he recovered his breath, drank for a few minutes under a cold tap, unpacked the cans in the projection booth upstairs and, his mission completed, returned to his post at the electrical workshop, an island in the middle of a spaghetti-junction of rail tracks outside the mineral crushing plant.

Since he also deposited the cans at the Huelva bus station for their return trip to Seville the day after the film's screening, Alonso made this journey twice a week – four times if there was a national holiday that merited a second film – and he did so every week of the year until, a decade later, they finally built a road bridge across the river, eliminating the need for him to travel at all.

The Cinema Corrales was built at the beginning of the 1950s by the Tharsis Sulphur and Copper Company. The company had actually built the whole village, which existed only because the company did. It was not the first Scottish-owned company to create a world around its mining interests in Southern Spain, since Rio Tinto had done so half a century earlier. Like Rio, Tharsis needed places to house its workers, and so it created them. When this was completed and the houses were occupied, the extent of the village's isolation became increasingly evident, so an infrastructure was gradually added, facilities designed to cement a sense of community and to keep the workers and their families functional – church, school, hospital, market, working men's club, and so on. Then someone suggested that a place of entertainment – a cinema, for example – might provide both a window on the world and a welcome distraction, one which in the long evenings before television reached rural Spain everyone in the village could share each week.

With its social mandate and limited budget, the cinema attempted to please everyone. There were the raucous Spanish folkloric comedy-dramas with flamenco interludes – usually featuring one of the trio of popular gypsy divas (Carmen Sevilla, Lola Flores, Paquita Rico) who reliably brought anyone still capable of movement out of their houses. There were the conservative and sentimental local comedies, with venerable comic actors (Manolo Moran, Miguel Ligero among them) and supporting cast chronically overacting, as if playing to an imaginary balcony. There would soon be the gaudy, song-punctuated period melodramas of the voluptuous Sara Montiel, and the anodyne musicals of child prodigies Joselito and Marisol. And there were the Mexican movies built around singing cowboys with unusually large hats such as Jorge Negrete, often with real-life sometime-wife Maria Felix in tow, riding past giant cacti; or the comedies of Cantinflas, whose strangely sparse moustache and baggy-trousered waddle prompted reflexive laughter in many, including for a moment the Hollywood studios, which gave him a disturbingly brief American career before sending him back to Mexico. In these films people at least spoke with their own voices, although it was not necessarily synchronised dialogue recorded at the same time as the picture: the dialogue was often added later, the actors invariably sounding shrill and declaratory, even in their own language. And when my friends and I "played" at the film – acting out some crude, truncated pantomime version of it the following day – we always affected Castilian accents, because the film did. (Striving for maximum authenticity in these re-enactments, I once asked a seamstress in the village to replicate Clark Gable's fringed buckskin jacket from *Across the Wide Missouri*. It wasn't buckskin – some heavy, khaki-coloured cotton had to do, but it did have fringes.)

But many of the films shown in the village had started life years earlier in a different country in another language, and it was with these that Spanish dubbing entered a realm of its own. Low literacy at this time meant that many cinemagoers were reluctant or unable to read subtitles, so the dialogue in all foreign films was spoken by Spanish actors and the principle accepted – even welcomed – by audiences. Every word was dubbed into Spanish except for the songs in musicals, which would have been impossible to replicate with any authenticity or conviction. Even Tarzan's yodel had a perceptibly Hispanic cadence to it, and his primitive communication methods simply reinforced the idea of language being somehow insignificant. Most of the foreign movies shown at the Cinema Corrales were American, although there was one British film programmed by the cinema during those years, the Ealing comedy *The Lavender Hill Mob*, which played to an empty house on a stormy night. Overseas stars often had the same voice – usually that of a well-known stage actor – dubbing their Spanish in a succession of films, and since the objective was to keep the language as neutral and as devoid of nuance as possible (no regional accents were heard except in comedies), this meant that John Wayne's open-range voice was dubbed with mannered theatricality by the Spanish equivalent of John Gielgud. So comprehensively did this ventriloquism take hold that when American actors began visiting the country themselves, it was a life-changing disillusion for some to discover that Burt Lancaster couldn't really speak Spanish. (Spain was not alone in its dubbing custom, which was practiced in many countries. When he was still a film critic, the director François Truffaut remarked on the absurdity of the cowboys addressing each other as "monsieur" in the French-dubbed version of Nicholas Ray's *Johnny Guitar*, but that this helped to emphasise the film's inherent theatricality.)

Not only did these actors have no opportunity to talk for themselves in their films; in the village we even made up our own variations of their names. Disregarding how these might have been pronounced in their country of origin, we twisted and redefined their identities into phonetic Andaluz, as if they all lived locally and worked in the mines. Thus John Wayne became HON-BAENE and Burt Lancaster BOOR-LANCATHTER, while Rock Hudson contracted easily into RO-OODSON. Johnny (HONI) Weissmuller's surname was too difficult to adapt and he only played one role anyway: Tarzan, or rather TAR-THAN, with the stress on the second syllable.

Since we were still less than halfway through the nearly four decades of Franco's dictatorship, dubbing also enabled some films to be cleared by the censors only if lines of foundation-shifting dialogue were added when characters were not on screen or had their backs to the camera. In John Ford's 1953 movie *Mogambo*, for example, a frosty and demure Grace Kelly – recently married and on an African safari with her husband Donald Sinden – becomes irresistibly infatuated with hunter and guide Clark Gable, to Sinden's understandable displeasure. Since such behaviour by a woman was considered unacceptable in 1950s Spain, the relationship between the couple was simply changed. An off-camera speech was added in the dubbing to emphasise that Kelly was engaged to a man back in England, and that Sinden's indignation was prompted by the fact that he was the best friend of the British fiancé, on whose behalf he was chaperoning her.

Inside the first can of each film was the *hoja de censura*, a single folded parchment page in an envelope. On one side, decorated with stamps and seals, was the official certification, declaring the age restrictions on the film's audience – those for whom it was, as they put it, *autorizada*. Since the weekly film was the only entertainment available in the village, there was a corresponding reluctance to exclude anyone from attending, so the cinema rarely took any notice of this. I once got to see Lee Marvin pour burning coffee over Gloria Grahame in *The Big Heat* at the age of seven, but occasionally they would remember to enforce the classification and I would be advised to stay away, or to remain in the projection booth where nobody could see me.

On the other side of the page was a list of the cuts and changes the distributor was obliged to make before the film could be shown at all: kisses to be abbreviated or eliminated, lines of dialogue to be added or subtracted, and occasionally – as with *Mogambo* – a key plot modification. All of these were clearly outlined, with precise references to reel number and scene. An entire sequence might be excised – as was the case with Liliane Montevecchi's musical striptease involving bananas in *King Creole*.

When a few years ago the Spanish Filmotheque sent me a compilation of screen moments deleted by distributors on the censor's orders from 1957 to 1977, titled *Corten 40 Metros de Chinos* ("Cut 40 Metres of Chinese People", an instruction epitomising the capricious absurdity of state censorship), I was unexpectedly overwhelmed, watching it through astonished tears like the character played by Jacques Perrin at the end of *Cinema Paradiso*, when he screens a reel of censored kisses edited together and bequeathed to him by his childhood mentor, the village projectionist.

Cinema Corrales was in effect my own Cinema Paradiso, airlifted from Sicily to the south of Spain. Now a cultural centre that hosts theatrical performances, concerts, talks, art exhibitions, flamenco shows and conferences – a hybrid inconceivable at the time I am describing – the cinema became both the vortex of village life and the place where one first developed the idea of there being a world outside it.

It is said that you spend your adult years trying to justify the time you invested in your childhood obsessions, and this has proved to be so. My path to becoming a cinephile was an unswerving one; triggered by circumstance, following its steady course untroubled by distraction, a state in which initial intoxication gave way to growing addiction, then satisfied saturation and, finally, total surrender.

It is impossible to overestimate the power that Hollywood images of a parallel universe had on the viewer in so remote a setting. Although the cinema's programming was punctuated by the occasional rural drama, for the most part realism was subordinated to exoticism, adventure or glamour – the western landscapes (later to be shot in Spain itself), the hard shiny US cities, the palatial interiors of imagined houses, Lana Turner gliding down a spiral staircase in white sequins and tulle, John Wayne crossing a boundless Arizona plain on horseback without complaint, the never-ending succession of ropes that Tarzan used to swing through the jungle, the enormous American cars that resembled spaceships. It was the cars which probably had the greatest impact of all, since there were none at all in our world, and even if there had been, there was nowhere to go in them, except along a dusty track to a neighbouring village. You had to cross the river to Huelva to see a car, and when you did none of the ones you saw looked like a spaceship.

The fact that the cinema's budget and location did not allow it much programming flexibility meant that it was obliged to take "packages" of films from the various Spanish distributors, and since at that time actors and directors were usually under contract to Hollywood studios whose Spanish subdivisions therefore took care of all their local releases, it meant there was a surprisingly concentrated education in American cinema for an eager young film enthusiast who was paying attention. Within the same year I would see pictures directed by Otto Preminger, Jules Dassin, Anthony Mann and so on, noting their names and the Spanish titles of their movies. I had a book listing the filmographies of every Hollywood star, which enabled me to work out the original titles of films I knew only under their Spanish ones. The method I employed, primitive but effective, was to scrutinise the resumés of the relevant actors and identify which title they all had in common. So with *Una Vida Por Otra* ("One Life For Another") – with Robert Taylor, Ava Gardner, Howard Keel and Anthony Quinn – I could see that Taylor and Gardner had appeared in several films together, but in only one that featured Keel and Quinn as well. This was *Ride, Vaquero!*, directed by John Farrow, a case of a foreign film with a Spanish word already in its title (as in *Viva Zapata!*) being disregarded in favour of a bland substitute. Conversely *Reign of Terror*, an Anthony Mann movie set during the French Revolution, was exactly translated to *Reinado del Terror*, as were *Vorágine* for Preminger's *Whirlpool* and *Yo Confieso* for Hitchcock's *I Confess*, but *Lust for Life*, Vincente Minnelli's biopic of Van Gogh with Kirk Douglas in a constant artistic lather, mysteriously metamorphosed into *El Loco del Pelo Rojo* ("The Madman with the Red Hair"), an improbable contender for the tag line of a future Van Gogh retrospective.

Some of these films, old in the first place, were on their last gasps by the time they reached us. Having passed through a thousand projectors, the prints certainly were. Even more ancient were the government-controlled newsreels routinely shown before them. Distributors evidently believed that people who lived in remote southern locations were so out of touch with the world that it wouldn't matter if the newsreel we were viewing at the cinema was from a different year, possibly a different era. In the village we saw filmed coverage of the coronation of Queen Elizabeth II almost two years after it took place.

The cinema was a magical place grounded by familiar rituals. The manual checking of the print to ensure that a small sprocket tear would not lead to the spool becoming tangled in the projector; the assembling of the reels to enable us to show the film on one projector with two intermissions; the moments on the balcony outside the projection booth, from where we could watch the audience arrive; the sudden mass odyssey of men rushing into the small lobby to smoke frantically during the five-minute intervals between spools; the sound of sunflower seeds, the favoured film snack, being crunched underfoot; the bold, super-saturated colours and flourishes of the poster art for the film we were showing, designed initially to have an impact across the giant painted facades of big-city cinemas, then reduced down to poster size. Since these posters were later used to wrap the film cans for their return journey, the only way I was able to keep them was by replacing them with the brown wrapping paper I acquired from my father's office, an exchange which would later take place in conspiratorial silence in Pepe Dávila's electrical workshop.

Pepe Dávila was the silver-haired, softly-spoken manager of the cinema and his son – also Pepe Dávila, in the Spanish tradition of sons being named after their fathers – was the head projectionist. The young Pepe – taller, stronger, gentler, more educated and less combustible than most of the men in the village – worked as an electrician under his father, and on film nights he would teach me how to fire up the cinema's high-powered carbon-arc lamp on the projector, and to thread and load the first spool through the winding labyrinth it had to pass on its way through the shaft of light. His assistants were his brother-in-law Fernando and cousin Faustino. This was my first experience of a family business, or certainly of one to which I wanted to belong. (Village life also carried the misfortune of a family routinely inheriting a father's nickname. One man was called *El Sucio* – the Filthy One – on account of his poor personal hygiene, so his otherwise unsoiled wife and children were given variations on this – *La Sucia, Los Sucios* – like a bad smell passed down a family chain.)

The cinema had one liability: it was unable to show films photographed in CinemaScope. By the time I discovered movies, the first attempts at 3D had been and nearly gone, but widescreen CinemaScope, and the numerous variations which followed it, were clearly here to stay – except at Cinema Corrales, whose rigid 1.37:1 ("academy") aspect ratio screen could not have been replaced without substantial structural changes to the building itself. Fortunately, during the summer months, there was somewhere else to go.

Punta Umbría was a fishing village which became a resort town in summer, a few miles downriver from Huelva, at the place where the river met the sea. If you drove to it along the coast road from Portugal – which few did – you left your car on the edge of town, because there were no roads within it. Instead there were pavements and wooden pathways through the sand, best avoided in the heat of the day, when barefoot contact with it would strip a layer of skin from the soles of your feet. When I was three years old, walking along holding a toothbrush with a Mickey Mouse figure on the handle, I fell on a paving stone and cut open my forehead, requiring a rapid trip to the doctor and several stitches. For years later, whenever I followed the route we had taken to the surgery, I searched the sand in vain for residual signs of my blood.

Favoured as a holiday destination by wealthy families from around the south who could afford to escape the suffocating summer heat of inland Andalucia, it was also a place where a well-known bullfighter might recover from a goring or a rising soccer star might keep a yacht. Working fathers with holidaying wives and children, would catch the Friday evening ferry down from Huelva for the weekend, greeted by their families at the small pier on the riverside, while exhausted day trippers lined up for the return journey. Other than at *siesta* time, the jetty was always busy, full of people welcoming arrivals and waving off departures; supplies for the town were unloaded, children swam around the boats and waved at the passengers.

It resembled accounts of what St Tropez was like in the mid-1950s before celebrity, greed, overpopulation and loss of identity colluded in suffocating it. The ice cream stalls in the adjacent square were where I simultaneously discovered not only ice cream itself but an empathy with the underdog bordering on the pathological. There were two rival kiosks located next to each other – the Onubense and El Valenciano. The prosperous-looking, well-groomed, socially-fluid groups taking an evening stroll together, lambswool jumpers draped around the shoulders or tied at the waist, invariably purchased their ice cream cones – or their *horchatas* or *granizadas* – at the Onubense, with its convivial host and perceived superiority. The uningratiating little man with the sad eyes and protruding teeth who stood silently awaiting customers behind the counter at El Valenciano had an air of bruised melancholy unusual in a shopkeeper, so naturally I always went to him and encouraged others to do likewise.

Punta Umbría cast a particularly strong spell when there was a full moon, which illuminated the river, the sea and the adjacent marshland. The current in the river was so strong that if you floated down it on your back as the tide went out you arrived at the sea in a few minutes, the ocean waves slowly washing over you, checking and neutralising your movement. It was a catalyst for romantic yearning, the warm fragrance of the air and its bewitching mix of aromas opening up a young man's dream world.

There were two teenage sisters, who both resembled the French actress Jacqueline Sassard, living in a big wooden house on the riverside in the shade of a giant palm tree and an overgrown garden with a constant chorus of cicadas. Perceptibly more sophisticated than the village girls I knew, they were – with their ponytails and jeans and bare feet and alluring air of disengagement – what I hoped might await me as I stumbled towards adolescence.

They were part of a larger group of slender, stylish young men and women who spent their summers in Punta Umbría, meeting in various configurations at cool, quiet places by the river, and bathing there. Families with young children would instead settle for a few hours under protective awnings on the long, wide Atlantic Ocean beach, which as lunchtime approached was patrolled by boys from the village walking along the sand, selling homemade potato chips from baskets around their necks. The timing of their consumption, at the peak of the hunger following a morning's swimming, took these chips into realms of delirium.

It was in this place, for two months in the summer, that I was able to see films in CinemaScope. There were two permanent open-air cinemas operating during the season – the Cinemar San Fernando and the Pescadores – and for one indelible summer they were joined by a third, the Ria, whose seating consisted simply of wooden chairs in the sand on the banks of the river, gentle waves from the wash of the passing fishing boats lapping up to the makeshift bamboo fence. Because none of these venues could begin showing their films until after dark, I learned how to stay up late. Although not in CinemaScope, *Duel in the Sun* had a tremendous impact on me – as apparently it did on a child Martin Scorsese – and the Spanish translation of Niven Busch's novel, using the same artwork as the film poster, had me standing spellbound outside the window of the only store in the village that sold books. At the beach cinemas that summer, I saw everything that played, watching in wonderment two Samuel Fuller CinemaScope movies (*Hell and High Water, House of Bamboo*) and Howard Hawks's Egyptian epic *Land of the Pharaohs*, and on most mornings I walked to the Cinemar San Fernando to check what new flyers, with their miniaturised poster art, had come in on the boat from Huelva, to add to my collection.

It was also in Punta Umbría that I first saw *The Man Who Never Was* – significantly, because it was on the ocean beach there that a body was discovered in a celebrated incident of military deception during World War 2, when in 1943 British Intelligence left the body of a dead man – a homeless Welshman who had committed suicide – dressed as a naval officer, to float ashore. In the pockets of this waterlogged decoy, among fabricated letters and other documents of an invented personal life, were papers which revealed Allied plans to make beach landings in Greece and Sardinia – rather than in Sicily, which is where they would really take place. The body was taken upriver to Huelva for examination. The Germans, who enjoyed the support of Spain's fascist government, could barely believe their luck – until, of course, the Allied landings happened in Sicily and took them by surprise. Some claim that this changed the course of the war.

It seems remarkable now that the filmmakers should have gone all the way to the actual beach where the body was found, but they did, for reasons of both practicality and authenticity, since in the next scene we see the body being carried through the streets of nearby Huelva, where it was really taken. Puritano – the man who ran the motorboat service across the river from Corrales to Huelva – was cast as the fisherman who finds the body and reports it to the authorities, becoming in the process our first, and only, local movie celebrity. Whenever the film was shown in the area, there were cheers of recognition from the audience, because anybody who had ever crossed that river knew him.

When I finally saw my first English-language film on a visit to Scotland, it was Robert Aldrich's western *Vera Cruz*: a revelatory moment, but also a confusing one. Of course, there was the matter of adjusting to actors speaking in their own language with their own voices. But what was more striking was the reinforcement of the idea that, like Gregory Peck in *Duel in the Sun*, it was the amoral opportunist who held your attention. Burt Lancaster, dressed all in black, was the duplicitous adventurer who ran mischievous rings around Gary Cooper's paragon of integrity. Lancaster smiled constantly, revealing the whitest teeth in the American west – a dazzling but unsettling smile that I had never seen in a screen villain before, which added to the incongruity. He had the charm, swagger, magnetism, fearlessness and athletic flourish that one usually associated with the hero. It was rather like watching Errol Flynn in *The Adventures of Robin Hood* – a territory Lancaster himself briefly colonised in *The Flame and the Arrow* and *The Crimson Pirate* – except that the dashing philanthropist had become a self-interested scoundrel.

By then, my film odyssey was clearly under way, my curiosity and infatuation irreversible. It was evident that something extraordinary and enduring had happened in the projection booth at the Cinema Corrales, and then under the stars in Punta Umbría. Uncertainty might lie ahead, but a flaming torch had been lit and would illuminate the years that followed.

CHAPTER TWO

Corrales was a village so isolated that in order to give birth to me my mother required three different kinds of transport – a locomotive, a motorboat and a taxi – to reach a maternity hospital only six kilometres across the river and marshland from her home.

My father David was the fifth of six children growing up in the small mining community of Thorniewood, beyond the southern suburbs of Glasgow. Beginning as a mining surveyor, he worked long hours in rows only three feet high, the smell of the moleskin trousers he wore in such airless confinement prompting a constant nausea which reinforced his latent claustrophobia. As his aspirations grew and local employment opportunities diminished, he travelled by cargo ship to the south of Spain in 1930 to work as an engineer for a Scottish-owned mining company. It was his first journey outside the Glasgow area, to a destination now comparable in its remoteness with Central Africa, and as the ship made its way up the River Odiel after a turbulent few days at sea, he awoke early one morning to discover a very foreign country outside the porthole of his cabin. Passing the spot from where Columbus had set sail for America some centuries earlier, docking at the port of Huelva, and absorbing the extraterrestrial strangeness of where he found himself, he was driven for several hours along roads and dirt tracks to the villages of Tharsis, Calañas and La Zarza, the trio of mines around which his new employers had built their company. Primarily they mined pyrites, a compound of copper and sulphur that was sold both in an integrated form and broken down into its component parts.

Although the other expatriate engineers and their wives socialised together, it could be a lonely life after the working day was over if, as my father did, you confined yourself to the occasional glass of sherry. Time passed. My mother Marion – the eldest of three sisters, known to everyone as Minnie – was a schoolteacher from Bellshill, a neighbouring Lanarkshire town, whom he had been courting, as it was then called, in the months before leaving Scotland. He missed her, and so wrote her a letter, in perfect handwriting, declaring his strong feelings, proposing marriage and asking her to share his life in this improbable faraway place. He made it clear that he did not encourage or expect a response until she had experienced this world for herself, which she was unable to do until the school summer holidays, since only these months would enable her to be absent from work for sufficient time. But eventually she made the journey, and at the end of her stay decided that she would join him in this remote bubble, with its extreme heat, its forbidding solitude, and its impenetrable language. Returning to Scotland, she resigned from her teaching post and, at the end of the following term, packed her cases and travelled back to Spain. Two young Scots embarking on another life in a place far from home, they married in Seville, the most romantic of cities, their wedding photo taken under an orange tree.

Together they lived through the Spanish Civil War as sidelined aliens in a village quickly occupied by Franco's Nationalists. They became witnesses to the conflicts between families and to the betrayals within them, attempting to walk a benevolent tightrope across a vortex of internecine hostility. Well into World War 2, my father, alone among the engineer *émigrés* of the mines, went off to his own war, joining the British army at the age of 36 and sent to Italy, while my mother waited in various locations in England and

Scotland with my sister Lesley, then two years old. When it was over they returned to Spain, now an increasingly poor and isolated country, its despised dictatorship making it a pariah among the recovering democracies of Western Europe. They moved from the mines themselves to the other end of the railway track, Corrales, where the mineral was processed, crushed and loaded on to ships. In doing so, they became one of only two foreign couples living in the village, and my sister and I the only foreign children. It was a comfortable life, but a frustrating, uncomprehending environment for a small boy – born there, knowing no other world, speaking with the dense Andaluz accent of the region, yet also an outsider with a fluctuating sense of belonging, the son of the village's head mining engineer who, although from a modest background himself, was their employer and a foreigner.

I was taught at home by my mother, in a class of one, for several hours each morning. Pupils at the village school, which I briefly insisted on attending because my friends did, started the day by singing the Falangist anthem and pledging allegiance to Franco, which my parents correctly concluded might be a confusing and unwelcome indoctrination for a boy eventually destined for a Scottish boarding school. Being eight years older than me, my sister was already attending one of these by the time I became conscious of her absence from the house.

The inevitability of this – the certain knowledge that I would be forced to leave home soon after my ninth birthday – haunted my early childhood, punctuating it with dread. My home, it seemed clear to me, was the village, where all my friendships and memories were. The place that my mother and father referred to as "home" was in reality somewhere quite far away – the west of Scotland, from where they had come and to where, many years later, they would return.

By the separatist standards of the other expatriate mining engineers and their families, my parents were integrationists, adjusting their Glaswegian ways to their Spanish environment. They learned to speak the language, my father with academic precision, my mother with a gentle Scots cadence that charmed and amused; they were interested in the life of the village and respectful – if, in my father's case, a little remote – in their relationships with its people; they ate the range of food available in rural post-war Spain, restricting themselves each year to one trunk full of idiosyncratically British groceries (jelly powder, fish paste, HP sauce, Penguin biscuits) which came by ship from Glasgow. They saw no irregularity in dining on *paella* and shepherd's pie on successive nights, no anomaly in a devotion to Spanish soccer and an absorption in British periodicals, several of which they subscribed to. Yet they never lost their fundamental foreignness, just as I never lost my desire to belong there.

There were myths and assumptions about *los ingleses*, generated by the villagers' observations of my father and his colleagues up the railway line, and intensified by the very restricted sample of outsiders to whom they were ever exposed. These British people ate carrots and beetroot (true), vegetables rarely consumed even by those villagers who grew them. They had big feet – not true in the case of my father, although the steel tips he added to the soles of his shoes for durability over rugged terrain made his feet *sound* big. And they were godless heathens. Catholicism was the only branch of Christianity known in the village, so it followed that Protestants such as my parents must be protesting against Christ.

Catholicism was so completely dominant in Spanish life during the Franco years that it closed the door on any other form of worship. It is far from the only religion to have used fear as a form of social control, but this was a government which understood that its rule was reliant on an unyielding coalition of church and military, with the priest and the head of the Civil Guards joining the mayor and the doctor as the undisputed authority figures of towns and villages across the country.

Neither was the power of the Catholic church at all new to Spain. After ruling the country for around seven centuries, the Moors were finally expelled in 1492 by King Ferdinand and Queen Isabella, marking the beginning of the Inquisition and the so-called *Reconquista*, when an unremitting new religious fanaticism led to, among other events, thousands of Jews being forced to convert to Catholicism or be burned at the stake.

It was the perpetuation of this fervour which led to the inception of the *Semana Santa* (Holy Week) processions, a bizarre and extravagant ritual conceived by the church in the aftermath of the Inquisition and expanded over the years to focus attention on the events leading up to Jesus Christ's death, with penitents dressed in robes and hoods, dripping melting wax from giant candles as they walked, accompanying religious statues carried through the streets by unidentifiable barefoot men with chains around their ankles, to the beat of a drum and the wail of lament. This surreal pagan pageantry – a compelling manifestation of the continuing power and influence of the church, and a hallucinatory punctuation mark of my childhood – is still in evidence in much of Spain at Easter, nowhere more so than in Seville.

Seville is the Spain of seductive, feverish folklore. Although Andalucia was colonised in turn by Greeks, Phoenicians, Carthaginians, Romans and Vandals – making it, over the centuries, perhaps the most invaded area of all Europe – it was the Moors who stayed the longest and left the most indelible imprint. There are other southern cities which just as arrestingly represent the country's Arabic/Islamic roots – Córdoba with its Mezquita and Granada its Alhambra may have the best examples of North African art and architecture anywhere in the world outside of North Africa itself – but it is Seville which most strikingly synthesises the magic and mystery of its Arab heritage.

Perhaps because Huelva never felt like a city – just a town with its own province – Seville always seemed a kind of exotic, exhilarating hothouse, a place of enchantment. It began in the villages and countryside one travelled through to reach it – the small whitewashed houses; the intoxicating fragrance of orange blossom, of bougainvillea and oleander and wisteria; the rough, arid earth; the almond trees and olive plantations; the bright sun and cool shadows; sometimes, against a bare horizon, the silhouetted outline of a bull-shaped billboard advertising Osborne brandy. Once you were there, the seduction escalated – the Islamic gardens with fountains; the wrought iron gates lined with geranium and jasmine; the aromatic waves, the hum of the city in the early evening light; the sound of flamenco drifting out of bars and courtyards; and, incessantly, cicadas, the recurring element in the soundtrack of the south.

A remarkable mix architecturally (the perfect minaret of the Giralda, the Alcazar palace), Seville also had tremendous style and spirit, never more potently than during the April fair, which emerged from the deep slumber and foreboding silence of Easter as if someone had opened the shutters on the world and let in the music and light. For seven days it ran (and continues to do) from noon until the following morning, and then a few hours later it started again. People dressed as they would at no other time of the year: the women in polka-dotted flamenco dresses, the men in short embroidered jackets and high-waisted trousers, together resembling folkloric cartoons. By day there were horses and parades and bullfights; by night, drinking and dancing under fairy lights and bunting, beautiful girls with perfect postures performing *Sevillanas* in pavilions, the accompanying singers and syncopated claps in seamless support. Then, in the early light, groups of revellers slowly walking home, families eating *churros* and drinking hot chocolate together, old ladies in black sighing into their fans, waving around the warm morning air.

Flamenco is only a component of the *feria*, but a significant one. Its demonstrative swagger tempered with mournful introspection, flamenco is certainly capable of lapsing into melodrama and posturing, but it comes from an unswervingly emotional core. It's about feeling – *only* about feeling – and about the declaration of that feeling. It is the soul music of Spain, with a cloud of North African dust scattered over it. It enters the bloodstream of young Spaniards at an early age and never leaves. Everyone in the south, of whatever age, seems to be good at it – singing, dancing, clapping – for the most fundamental of reasons: it is in their systems.

Seville was also the place of greetings and goodbyes. When I was leaving home to travel to school in Scotland, as I would soon be doing, we invariably arrived in the city long before departure time, so there were several tearful hours to be spent wandering disconsolately around the Parque Maria Luisa, followed by an agonising goodbye dinner upstairs at the Riviera, a restaurant whose cosmopolitan air appealed to my father, who ate out about once a year. There smartly dressed local families and small groups of well-heeled travellers dined under large overhead fans, whose cool swish perfectly complemented the frosty discretion of the service. (On my last visit there, in 1961, the most convivial table was occupied by David Lean, Omar and Mrs Sharif, Anthony Quayle and various production personnel from *Lawrence of Arabia*, which was filming in Southern Spain at the time. It was the first time I had seen a table full of men wearing dinner jackets.)

In the lingering aftermath of the civil war, all of rural Spain suffered from a food shortage and in some places people went hungry, particularly in areas where they were unable to grow or kill their own food. Corrales was fortunate in being able to do both. There was plenty of arable land in the surrounding countryside, reliable rain in winter and an application of basic irrigation methods. Small orchards abounded and we were close to the sea, so fresh fish was always available. Hens, goats, sheep and pigs were raised for slaughter. Rabbits roamed the woods, the pigeons overhead. I was aware that some of my friends occasionally ate cats and so kept a watchful eye on my mother's pet one, and that *estás gordo* (you're fat) was considered a compliment, because if you were fat it meant you could afford to be. Bread, baked in the village and sometimes delivered to us by donkey, was a constant in the local diet – bread with everything, and for snacks in the late afternoon little loaves sliced down the middle, with olive oil and sugar, or with dark, dense chocolate, or with lard (butter was considered a costly indulgence), or with *tocino*, pig fat.

Despite the freshness and range of the food in the area, the civil war diet had left its imprint on the young men and women growing up at the time. Men in particular tended to be short and slight in build, so the few tall ones in the village were easy to identify at some distance. There was no local dentist and visits to the few practices in Huelva were expensive and time-consuming, so the condition of the villagers' teeth was usually terrible, particularly as they got older, when in some cases smiles became a checkerboard of dark spaces between the surviving teeth. I gave little attention to mine, and paid the price by losing several of them on my first encounter with a Scottish dentist.

For much of the day I lived, as solitary children do, in my own world. After morning lessons, my father would return home for lunch, then have a *siesta* in the armchair next to the large radio that blared out the BBC news followed by the children's programme *Listen With Mother*, which for a while I did, to the incomprehension of my village friends who did not listen to anything with their mothers. On some evenings, I would take a tepid bath with my father, who tested me on the capitals of the world, cities whose names I quickly learned to recite without hesitation or error, even though the world they represented seemed incomprehensibly far away. Then the two of them would read, listen to the radio, fill in the weekly Spanish football pools – discussing whether Bilbao might beat Valencia, or the reverse, or if a draw was more likely – while I played with my collection of model cars, among which my favourite was an Austin taxi, a vehicle I was yet to see life-size in its natural habitat, a British city street.

There was no telephone – only an internal line connecting the various mining villages and an office in Huelva via a company switchboard during office hours, so for the most part the house was almost sepulchral in its shade and quiet, particularly in the afternoons, when I would go walking alone in the countryside, up to the transporter, across to the sawmill, down to the marshes, over to the orange orchard.

Football was the only game played in the village, and on most Sundays we all wandered down to a pitch of dusty gravel – with a whitewashed wall around it, as if it were a proper stadium – and watched the local team play. If there was bad behaviour during a game – over-aggressive tackles prompting retaliatory punches – my father would stand up and walk out, feeling that by staying he was somehow condoning it. I was given a child's Barcelona team kit for my seventh birthday, and I recklessly gambled my father's tennis cups (and occasionally had to plead for their return, claiming a misunderstanding) to raise the stakes in games played on the mineral behind our house, the kind of surface on which a routine fall could open up your knee. Nearby there was a concrete tennis court, where my father began giving me lessons about five minutes after I learned how to walk. Sometimes on a Sunday morning, he took the motorboat across the river for a few sets against adult opponents at the Huelva tennis club, but golf, the game of choice among expatriates, was of no interest to him.

Unless it was a Sunday with a film or football match to attend, the days passed in a dreamy vacuum. Young children tend to invent improbable jobs for themselves. Mine was to work as a brakesman on the mineral wagons which travelled up and down the railway line from the mines themselves to the piers, where they were loaded on to ships: a full load one way, an empty wagon the other. A brakesman travelled with each wagon, adjusting their individual brakes to ensure that the load was secure and that there were no disruptive collisions if the engine pulling them had to make a sudden stop. The men performing this hazardous work – with the train at full speed a slip from their vulnerable perches could prove fatal – all wore black berets that smelled of the mineral they minded, so I coveted one of those as well, to go with the job for which I would remain ineligible until long after I no longer wanted it.

I often saw these wagons come and go – trying on berets while the mineral in the wagons was emptied and the engine was turned around – because I enjoyed sitting around the station, watching things happen. On Monday mornings the *viajero* came in, with its added passenger coach for people travelling down from the Tharsis mine for a day's shopping in Huelva, often to buy fabric, since many people made their own clothes. Each afternoon I collected the mail, most of it bearing foreign stamps. The weekly highlight was the arrival of the *Beano* and the *Dandy*, the British comics to which my parents subscribed to give me some grounding in Anglo pop-culture references I might eventually share with future boarding school friends, with whom I would otherwise have little in common. I had heard that serious, sensible boys of my age read the *Eagle*, which was favoured by parents who believed that comics should educate as well as amuse – but the sampling of a few issues revealed a stultifying worthiness.

Next to the station was the *cuartel* of the Civil Guards, whose tricorn hats have over the years become emblematic of Franco's dictatorship, the defining head gear of its protectors – even more so after one was worn by the man who in the late 1970s tried to lead a military coup against King Juan Carlos and the new democratic government by taking over parliament. The *cuartel* was the barracks where the Civil Guards and their families were all accommodated, and the headquarters out of which they operated. Living so close to it, and having several of their sons and daughters as my friends, it never occurred to me to question why there were so many roaming law enforcers in such a small village and its surrounding countryside. But the answer is clear: this is the way the country was run, particularly in rural areas considered potential hives of subversion. Ours – being close to the railways, ships, mines and other centres of activity that could be captured and controlled – clearly required close monitoring. At Christmas the courtyard of the *cuartel* became a kind of pop-up slaughter house – pigs hung upside down on ropes, their throats cut, bleeding all over the soil until they were dead and dry, ready to start being turned into a meal for the residents and their guests.

Animals either had a function or they were food. The function of a bull – bred as it was mostly for ceremony and combat – was quite specific. Its role was to be an essential element in a Spanish tradition, to provide entertainment for the thousands who attended the *corridas* in Huelva during the summer months, and then to die, since its sacrifice was a fundamental component of the event's climax. One of my father's work colleagues enjoyed bullfights and was sure that I would too, so occasionally we would cross the river, take a carriage ride up to the bullring and sit in the late afternoon shade as the noise and ceremony got under way around us, the dust rising as the horses began to move around the ring. It was my first exposure to a crowd of this size, all in a state of baying, adrenalized over-excitement, their effect both rousing and intimidating, intensified by the familiar flourishes of a small band playing *paso dobles*. My sympathies – entirely with the bull in the early stages, when there seemed to be so many people in the ring to provoke, debilitate and confuse it – began to shift as the afternoon moved into evening and the rituals became more spellbinding in the rising heat, and when it came to the final showdown – one man, one bull – it was difficult not to be moved by the primitive intensity of the encounter, whose staging in a large arena helps to define it as one of the last of the gladiatorial spectacles, in some parts of Spain now a vanishing one.

Crossing the river for *any* reason represented a kind of freedom which only those who have lived in isolation will understand. It now seems unthinkable that as children and young adolescents we would sometimes row a boat across it, given the distance of the crossing, the depth of the water and the ferocity of the tides. The governing principle was that you had to travel to whatever you were seeking, because it wouldn't come to you. The exception was the mid-summer festival of San Pedro, an annual event created by and for the village in honour of its patron saint. Its climax was a dance held on the *paseo*, a concrete square colonised in the summer months by groups of strolling young men and women displaying themselves to each other as courtship prospects. The *paseo* was outside the casino, the imposing whitewashed and tiled working men's club at the entrance to the village, where you could play billiards or dominoes and have a beer and a couple of anchovies on a toothpick for next to nothing.

The music for the dance was provided by a small band of middle-aged men in blue blazers, cream slacks and white moccasins, their hair immaculately brilliantined, their repertoire unyieldingly traditional – "Bésame Mucho", "Moliendo Café", "Perfidia", "Quizás, Quizás, Quizás", "Aquellos Ojos Verdes", "Te Quiero Dijiste", and so on. Cover versions of such songs in heavily accented Spanish would soon be recorded by foreign singers such as Nat King Cole and Cliff Richard, whose elongated vowels and eccentric stresses prompted affectionate, amused mimicry among Spanish listeners.

Tables and chairs were positioned around the square like a viewing gallery, enabling the developing intimacy of the dancing couples to be monitored by the surveillance of seated relatives. The women never smoked, rarely drank; the men invariably did too much of both. One cannot overstate the significance of slow-dancing in the carnal lexicon of the young who grew up amid the sexual repression in such villages, since it provided the only lingering, socially-sanctioned body contact available to the boys and girls who were not officially courting. Hormones in overdrive, these were the cherished moments of adventure and discovery for those who found themselves responding, although some might have to wait another year to relive the experience. By this time, of course, life would have moved on.

As indeed mine did. An awareness of the unavoidable rupture that awaited me and had acted as the dark pulse beat to my childhood was growing gradually but constantly. I would say goodbye to everyone in the village – working my way around all the houses and places of work – then leave Spain, and for the next nine years (in effect, my life so far again) attend two Scottish boarding schools – one west of Glasgow, one east of Edinburgh – seeing my mother and father for two months each summer and returning to Corrales every second one.

At first, the moment of truth, the immobilising pain of leaving – of watching my parents recede, and eventually disappear from sight, on the station platform in Seville as the train drew out – was a few months away. Then a few weeks. Finally, a few days.

Then, as if suddenly, I was gone.

CHAPTER THREE

In the muted afternoon sunlight of late summer in the west of Scotland – escorted by my mother, father and sister – I boarded a ferry in Greenock, a coastal town upriver from Glasgow, and sailed across the Firth of Clyde to Helensburgh, where my boarding school was.

Over a long holiday in Largs, the seaside resort favoured by my parents for their visits to Scotland, saturating myself in thrice-weekly visits to the Viking cinema, I had prepared for this moment so much, had anticipated it so vividly for so long, that when it finally came it felt as if it was being experienced by someone else, a different nine-year-old boy who would feel the ache of separation less. A brief tour of the schoolhouse and grounds was conducted. Homilies were exchanged, tears resisted, goodbyes said.

A bewildered numbness set in to neutralise the unrest. I imagined my family on their return journey across the water and down the coast, communicating fitfully, wearied by my distress. I would be sitting on my dormitory bed in pyjamas and dressing gown by the time they reached Largs. I didn't really understand what was going on, except for knowing that it was destined and irreversible. An unavoidable collusion of forces had taken me there, an early encounter in my lifelong fear of institutions and my resistance to uncontested authority.

The name of the school was Larchfield. On the first night I slept in a room full of boys I had only met half an hour earlier. When we woke in the morning each of us in turn fully immersed himself in an ice-cold bath, the character-building ritual that began each day.

At breakfast, over bowls of dense and lumpy porridge, I met boys from the other dormitories, most of them sons of parents who also lived abroad, which is why we were all there. More mysterious was the presence of children whose families resided in the UK, even in Scotland itself. Did their mothers and fathers not want them at home? Later we encountered the day boys, who lived locally and walked back to their houses in the afternoon after classes, so were living in a world quite different from ours.

I had little sense of what standard of student I might be. Solitary home schooling in a Spanish village had left me with no comparative point of reference, but it became evident that my mother had taught me well, and that childhood isolation had intensified my comprehension and memory. I was soon top of the class in several subjects, which raised my spirits, generated a sense of purpose, and dissipated the depression that might have otherwise have settled over me as I became increasingly aware of the life sentence I had just begun.

The single certainty in this germ-generating environment was that you would soon be immobilised by flu, which travelled unavoidably around the boarders with the speed of light. I had never experienced such illness before, so was unfamiliar with the bed-ridden discomfort which quickly followed, but it was this enforced stillness which introduced me to reading books. I had rarely done this in Spain, where the only novels I had read were Cervantes' *Don Quijote* and Ibáñez's *Blood and Sand*. The school dormitory substitutes for these great works were Enid Blyton's Secret Seven and Famous Five stories, with which I became completely absorbed. When my temperature rose to levels that required isolation treatment, I was moved to the heavily curtained "sick room", where a blue light was left on all night, and the reading continued.

My only school visitor was my sister Lesley, who occasionally travelled up from Glasgow to take me out on a Saturday afternoon. During the Christmas and Easter holidays, I stayed with my father's sister Peggy in Viewpark, a suburb south of Glasgow near the mining village where they had both grown up. At Christmas, a single gift from my parents via my aunt – a film annual, precision-wrapped in festive paper – awaited me, partially hidden in the pantry under the stairs. Each summer I saw my mother and father: Scotland one year, Spain the next.

The primary benefit of lodging at my aunt's was that there were three buses I could take to four destinations – Bellshill, Hamilton, Motherwell, Wishaw – which each had at least two cinemas. Once I had navigated the bus routes and numbers, and the money required for a cinema ticket and a return journey, I was travelling to see films every afternoon except Sunday. After the years of restricted viewing, I had multiple options. It never bothered me that I had no friends, because having no friends meant no obligations and more guilt-free time to watch movies, and since these were often double bills that now seem extraordinary (Stanley Kubrick's *Paths of Glory* and Don Siegel's *Baby Face Nelson* in the same programme), the abundance was exhilarating. It was a thrilling antidote to the regimentation of school – freedom to do what I wanted. It turned out that all I wanted was unlimited access to films.

I saw so many that I developed arcane theories about historical behaviour. One was that the reason Vikings became so quickly inebriated at celebrations of any kind is that they drank out of a horn rather than a goblet, and so could never put it down for a rest the way they might a glass or cup. It was always refilled immediately. The long scene of party debauchery early in Richard Fleischer's *The Vikings* conclusively reinforced this for me.

For the first time I also watched television, which was new to me because it hadn't yet reached southern Spain. If it had, I suspect it would've been dreary and propagandist, delivered in the fruity Castilian cadences we mocked in the south, except when it was televising soccer matches or bullfights. On the other hand, television in Scotland, with just two channels, was an intoxicating mix of programming for a young boy – a detective series (*Mark Saber*), a pirate series (*The Buccaneers*), five western series (*Maverick, Laramie, Cheyenne, Rawhide, Wagon Train*) and two mythological superhero series (*Robin Hood, William Tell*). The game shows (*Take Your Pick, Spot the Tune, Double Your Money*) were fascinating because the money and gifts you could win as a contestant would keep an entire Spanish village in food, drink and housing for a couple of years. I actually did win once – a substantial amount – if answers given in a living room and witnessed only by one's relatives qualified for prizes.

During that first freezing Scottish winter – whether living at school or at my aunt's – much of my energy went into seeking warmth, or at least into trying to diminish cold. It was remarkable how much time and concentration this occupied, and the amount of movement required not to become encrusted by it. The coldest part of me was my ears, so cold that little ridges began to form like icicles along their tips, the pain intensifying in consonance with the sliding temperature. Even colder were the buses, and the one from Glasgow to Viewpark was always packed with people breathing out entire clouds when they exhaled. One winter evening, my aunt and I travelled home from the city while on the upstairs floor a group played a spirited stripped-down version of Johnny Kidd and the Pirates' "Shakin' All Over", with acoustic guitars, foot stomps and feverish vocals. It was as close to the spirit of flamenco as I had ever heard outside Spain.

Travellers on this bus route could speak of little but the arrest of a serial killer named Peter Manuel. The area we travelled through, south of the city towards Lanarkshire, had for some time been the scene of his crimes, its people preoccupied and perturbed by numerous unsolved murders, and when Manuel was arrested and charged in the first few days of 1958, the talk on the bus became even louder. When he was found guilty of seven of these murders (and a couple of attributed but unproved ones) and hanged a few months later, the chatter became deafening. At some moment between his arrest and his hanging, I met a solitary boy in the local playground who claimed to be Manuel's young cousin. For a few days, we became playmates, to the uncomprehending disbelief of my aunt. Then, one day, he stopped coming. I never saw him again.

When I was about 11, I became increasingly reluctant to play sports. I decided I wasn't good at them, and that I didn't want to do things I wasn't good at, although this may have been a strategy I adopted to conceal fear and embarrassment. So I began to withdraw and to fabricate reasons not to play, feigning illness occasionally.

Eventually I didn't have to pretend at all. Returning from one of my two summer visits to Spain during my four years at Larchfield, I turned out to have jaundice. Within an hour of diagnosis, with an urgency which took me by surprise, an ambulance arrived to drive me to Ruchill, Glasgow's hospital for infectious diseases. In a boarding school environment, infectious diseases are particularly unwelcome, and jaundice would have set off every epidemic alarm bell. Requiring immediate segregation and never having been in a hospital, I was unloaded some time later in what appeared to be an enormous Victorian industrial estate with tall chimneys, a giant incubator of chronic sickness. Since I knew few people in Scotland and was perceived to be dangerous to the health of others, nobody came to see me except my sister and the school matron who had called the ambulance to take me there in the first place. During my two weeks of residence, I lay quietly in a large empty room on my own, immobile and unperturbed, reading and re-reading the few film magazines I had brought with me. Another boy in a neighbouring ward repeatedly called for the nurse, so following the mistaken assumption that all children crave company they wheeled in his bed to join mine. By then completely settled into my solitude, I did not respond well to his continuing shouts for attention at frequent intervals, so was silently relieved when he was returned to doing this from next door.

While convalescing at my aunt's house after being discharged, and going to see all the films I had been reading about during my time in hospital, I discovered a little more about the treatment of, and recovery from, jaundice. The most fundamental instruction, I learnt, was to avoid *all* fried foods under *any* circumstances. This was surprising since at the hospital, apart from breakfast cereal, there had hardly been a meal that wasn't fried. And if there was, chips came with it.

When I returned to school, I did so with buoyancy and renewed spirit, as if illness had purged me of fear, as if I had risen above my insecurities and vulnerability and created something worthwhile out of my isolation. Accordingly, I now began to play robust and dynamic rugby, winning the ball in the line outs, combative in the scrums, running purposefully, crashing through everybody and everything. Then, when my final summer at Larchfield came around, where I would once have stood on the boundary of the cricket field intoxicated by the smell of new-mown grass, I instead became a prodigious all-rounder, earning my team colours with a match-winning batsman's innings, and consistently bowling out the opposition. Somewhere in the rubble of the world – the school itself long closed – there is a cricket cup with my name engraved on it.

It was a short-lived triumph, but I relished it. In a vain attempt to extend my sense of accomplishment, I spent most of the daylight hours during the lengthy holiday which followed bowling at cricket stumps on our landlady's lawn in Largs, and rarely struck them. Inviting praise from my father – who was not a cricket player but understood the game's fundamental principle (ball must hit stumps) – he pointed this out as kindly as he could. It was textbook tragi-comic, affirmation-seeking, lonely-boy behaviour.

This was amplified by a change of school and coast – from Larchfield (west) to Loretto (east), which was located in Musselburgh, a few miles outside Edinburgh. At 13, I still had little experience of back seat car travel, and the winding country roads we took as we drove east across Scotland, compounded by the acrid smell of the vehicle's interior, led to several stops to relieve roadside nausea. One of the finest pop singles of all time – Elvis Presley's "His Latest Flame" – had been released only a few weeks earlier, and had already made its impact on me, so I quietly kept humming it to myself during the car ride, just for distraction.

Loretto's school motto was "Spartam nactus es, hanc exorna" – literally "Sparta is yours: adorn it", supposedly a mistranslation of a line in a play by Euripides which was really a reference to developing one's talent. However, Spartans were also a people who left their babies out on hillsides in sub-zero temperatures and force 10 gales, sanctifying the survivors and burying the dead. The school – with its complete absence of heating apart from a log fire in the evenings in the small school library – reflected this in the chilly environments of its numerous buildings.

This was solely a boarding school, its residents spread across several houses within walking distance of one another. Near the school's own spacious grounds were a gasworks and a large racecourse on which, in all my time there, I never saw a horse. Ferocious winds from the adjacent North Sea blew across it, compounding the desolation. In the other direction was the High Street, its centre of gravity an alluring ice cream parlour whose speciality was an enormous tower of fruit and ice-cream called a Knickerbocker Glory, a galaxy away from the small cones I had relished back in Punta Umbría. Across the road from this was an electrical shop with a small record counter which stocked only the top 20 chart singles and a few long-players. The wizened little lady who very competently operated this department had a remarkable idiosyncrasy which kept me spellbound in the course of my occasional purchases. When asked for a record – say, Dion's "Runaround Sue", one of the first singles I bought – she would, without turning around, lever her arm back to the shelf on which the discs sat – exactly like a jukebox arm – and whip the correct one on to the counter, as if she had eyes in her back, a contortionist's arm, and a magnet in her fingertips.

I was invariably accompanied to these places by my sister, who had moved from Glasgow to Edinburgh, where she worked as a receptionist at the Caledonian Hotel, with warm and comfortable staff lodgings up in the hotel's roof line near a chimney. Occasionally, if the wind was blowing in the direction of her open window in winter, smoke might come in, and once did for me. As I went into this next phase of purgatory, it was comforting to know that she was only a short bus ride away, and that I could sometimes use her room to change out of the kilt that was mandatory wear for Loretto boys on city excursions. Occasionally, when several of us travelled to Edinburgh together and were going on to a rugby match at Murrayfield, you could hear the unmistakable sound, almost in unison, of massed sporran chains hitting the floor of the bus terminal toilets.

Further reinforcing the Spartan motto, we also wore kilts all day on Sundays. The school had its own chapel, the crucifying dullness of whose services were compensated by its fabulous acoustics, the echo on the organ sound a particular highlight. There was a piece played quite regularly, Boëllmann's *Toccata* from *Suite Gothique*, which in its galloping rhythm and stirring bass notes struck me as the perfect foundation for a pop record. "Nut Rocker" by the improbably named B Bumble and the Stingers – an adaptation of the march from Tchaikovsky's *Nutcracker* – had been a recent No 1 hit in the UK, as had Jet Harris and Tony Meehan's "Diamonds". The latter was a non-classical piece, but an instrumental which featured bass guitar, as I imagined a pop adaptation of Boëllmann would, with its big-bad-bass rumble. The American guitarist Duane Eddy, one of whose albums was titled *The Twang's the Thang*, was also a reference point.

So I wrote to the pop music weekly *Record Mirror* – which had a readers' letters page – identifying the Boëllmann piece as something which should be heard, considered and perhaps revisited by pop-classical reinterpreters such as B Bumble and the Stingers. A few days later, a letter arrived for me – the first I'd ever received postmarked London – from someone called Kim Fowley, who informed me that he was B Bumble's arranger/producer, that he was interested in exploring my idea, and that I should send him a tape of what the music might sound like if performed by a group. As there was no existing one that I could enlist, I found a bass player, guitarist, organist and drummer within the school, played them a recording of Boëllmann's *Toccata*, and helped them to work out a primitive arrangement of it. Then I borrowed a reel-to-reel tape recorder, bought the single spool of tape I could afford, and encouraged them to go through the piece repeatedly until we felt there was a version worth sending before we ran out of tape. Finally, I boxed and posted it, together with an excited cover letter to Mr Fowley. Naturally, I never heard from him again. As my interest in pop music widened, his name began appearing regularly in news stories about bands, notably as the recruiter and manager of all-girl group The Runaways in Los Angeles in the 1970s.

Although in a boarding school all contact with the outside world is unnaturally intensified, this was not the birth of the schoolboy entrepreneur in me, but rather an indicator of how infatuated I could become with an idea and how determined I was to follow through on it. Good ideas – properly explored and executed – seemed to be at the pulse of all worthwhile creative activity. I've never been interested in business except as a way of enabling such ideas to come fully to life. And, of course as a means of ensuring that everybody involved is rewarded for their accomplishments. But the actual mechanics of business are really of little interest to me. Enthusiasm, I suppose, is an energy in itself, because it generates activity.

Shortly after my 17th birthday I was expelled from school. There was a time-honoured custom among the older bad boys – among whom I now counted myself – that after completing exams, a few of us would climb out of our hall of residence through an unlocked ground floor window late at night and wander around the school grounds smoking cigarettes and drinking alcohol, two of the categorically forbidden activities in the school's bulging lexicon of them. Then, in the morning, one could count on a few witnesses discreetly spreading the word to ensure some added lustre to one's outlaw status. So, with a packet of Benson & Hedges and a small bottle of Martell brandy, one night two weeks before the end of term, another boy and I did exactly this. I had thought that the staff, while aware that such things sometimes went on, turned a blind eye to banal celebratory hi-jinks. But halfway across the lawn behind the chapel, several hundred yards from our house, a schoolmaster's torch shone in our faces and we were done for.

The other boy was soon to leave school anyway, so this simply accelerated his departure. For me – with a year still to go – a surprising proposal was made. Since my parents had no phone in Spain, the headmaster first sent my father a telegram, then followed it with an "aerogram" going into more detail about what I had done and what my punishment was to be. To make an example of me, and discourage other boys from emulating my bad behaviour, I would stay away from school for half of the following autumn term and return in November. In effect, I was expelled for half a term. During the journey back to Scotland to begin his summer holiday, my father had an enlightened idea: that I should spend that time in Paris working for a shipping company that he had dealings with, and become fluent in French.

I arrived in Paris in mid-August. It was as empty as tradition had it at this time of the year, but there were still people working, including those in the company that employed me. I stayed in a little room in a hotel on the Boulevard Saint Marcel, and every morning I walked to work at a building on the Seine quayside across the road from the Gare d'Austerlitz. When not witnessing conversations in the office, I accompanied executives on their business meetings around the city, constantly exposed to French language wherever I went. In my first days there, the only place where I heard English spoken was in classes at the Alliance Française in Montparnasse, and this was only because we were being taught how to say the same thing in French.

It was there that I met Madeleine, a British girl from Royal Leamington Spa, a town name which, if it didn't exist already, one might imagine in an early English heritage film. She was a year older than me – significant at that age – intelligent and pretty and adventurous company as we discovered Paris together. By then in early September, the city was at its most unremittingly romantic, with a heightened, cartoonish lustre about it, as if delivering to order. We explored all the usual places, and also found some unexpected ones, such as the wonderful Allée des Cygnes, the island walkway in the middle of the Seine starting at the Bir-Hakeim bridge (under which a brooding, broken Marlon Brando would wander seven years later in the opening scene of *Last Tango in Paris*), with benches along the way to sit and dream, the spectral ubiquity of the Eiffel Tower, and the river and its traffic flowing past on both sides.

Sometimes at weekends we would spend the entire night out – walking around areas of interest, in late shows at cinemas, in bars around the old Les Halles market, in a Pigalle strip club, in a sleeping bag in the Bois de Boulogne, wherever our curiosity took us. One Sunday morning, we parted company outside a Metro station to return to our respective lodgings, hers north-west, mine south-east. Struggling without success to avoid sleep, I awoke at the end of the line in an otherwise empty carriage. I remained on board as the train turned around, aware that in the other direction there were only six stations until it reached mine, Then, incredulously, I came to at the *other* end of the line. For the third attempt, I decided to stand up for the the whole journey – and still, leaning against a pole, I managed to fall asleep. By this stage, there were enough other passengers to ask one who was travelling beyond my station to alert me. I finally crawled into bed with grateful surrender, relieved to avoid continuing this Kafkaesque daymare.

It was a glorious time of pleasure, carelessness and discovery. It felt as if everything was opening up – and the world was expanding to accommodate it. Then, at the end of October, halfway through the academic term, my penance and penalty paid, I resumed life as a schoolboy.

During the summer months and my subsequent absence, some significant construction work had been completed at the school. I was pleased to discover that final year students, as I now was, had been allocated single studies with beds, with the corresponding privacy this suggests. So, there was no dormitory chit-chat to contend with when I got back. As the returning expelled pupil who had paid his dues uncomplainingly and the international man of mystery who had made productive use of his time away, I was glad to be left alone to settle back in at my own pace. My status was never higher, and my curiosity and independence were beginning to flourish. The golden age of pirate radio was well under way, and my hours of study each day were punctuated with wonderful new records, played repeatedly. You would be certain to hear both sides of the new Beatles single "Day Tripper" / "We Can Work It Out" every half hour, as you would the Rolling Stones' "Get Off My Cloud", Wilson Pickett's "In the Midnight Hour" and the Walker Brothers' "My Ship is Coming In". But, in the receding daylight and shrinking temperatures of the encroaching Scottish winter, the record I could never listen to often enough was "California Dreamin" by the Mamas and Papas, with its freshness, its intoxicating harmonies and its promise of sunny days to come.

The comically prosaic name of the young English teacher who made the final terms at Loretto more stimulating for me was JB Smith. Although he had been present during the previous year, he was the kind of ally I wish I had found earlier in my schooling, because then I believe I would have been a more engaged, more effective student. He understood how to excite the imagination with a phrase or an insight, to be provocative and argumentative in exploring a subject, and to make connections between things that would awaken a young student mind to the pleasures of learning. As well as being able to glide between the usual cultural reference points, he could also discuss Elvis Presley, whom I deified at the time, and explain why his 1965 soundtrack album *Girl Happy*, for which I was an enthusiastic apologist, was entirely devoid of the vitality I ascribed to it – and he was right. He once took me to a Sunday afternoon talk in one of those old cultural-signalling Edinburgh terrace houses at which it became evident that the speaker, the Scots actor John Cairney, whose fame lay mostly in having played Robert Burns in a well-known one-man show (others were to follow), had enjoyed a very liquid lunch, which he continued in our company, becoming increasingly belligerent as the afternoon wore on. As we left, Mr. Smith lamented Cairney's self-sabotage: "Why did he do that?"

Then he talked to me about supplementing the starchy epic usually selected as the annual school play with *The Zoo Story*, a one-hour, one-act piece by Edward Albee about two men who meet on a bench in Central Park. One is a mild-mannered publishing executive and family man, the other an aggressive loner who just won't stop talking. The latter has what was then the longest soliloquy outside of Shakespeare. Did I want to play him?

I was already familiar with Albee's *Who's Afraid of Virginia Woolf?*, the film version of which was just about to be released, but even this didn't prepare me for the staggering intensity of the writing and the vivid freshness of the dialogue itself. All the good energy that emerged from my Paris interlude later went into rehearsing and performing *The Zoo Story*, an extraordinary experience which gave me a sense of accomplishment I had rarely felt, and which would later prompt me to continue this path at university.

Despite a withering final report, a checklist of frightful character flaws from an exasperated housemaster, when school was irreversibly over – exams finished, university place assured, farewells concluded – I felt, for the first time in the nine years I had devoted to it, that I had made some friends, that the sense of distance I had cultivated self-protectively since abandoning my Spanish home half a lifetime earlier and had allowed to deteriorate into anger and alienation, was over, and that the productive and positive parts of the school years had mostly been condensed into the final section.

After I walked out of the gates for the last time, I took a train to Yorkshire, where an end-of-school country house party, with overnight accommodation, was being hosted by the family of one of my new friends. It was the first party I had ever been invited to in Britain, and I was struck by the easy intimacy and interaction of the prosperous-looking boys and girls. There was a kind of debauched innocence about the way we all drifted towards someone we liked and paired up. It had the simple sweetness of promise, a gateway to a universe of options, the perfect coda to boarding school life.

I continued further south to London, which had a bewitching glow comparable to the one I had witnessed in Paris a year earlier. Strolling through Holland Park on a perfect summer evening, I heard on the transistor radio of a passer-by Los Bravos performing their UK Top 10 hit "Black is Black" – the first ever British hit by a Spanish band – interrupted by an announcer declaring that England had just won the soccer World Cup at Wembley Stadium. The country was completely alive, and so – about to hitchhike all the way home to Southern Spain – was I.

CHAPTER FOUR

Somewhere between Paris and Lyon, hitchhiking for the first time, I began to wonder why I had suddenly become irresistible to gay French motorists. Perhaps it was the fit of my white jeans, the quintessence of young male fashion in the summer of 1966. The first driver was a kangaroo-hopping priest – his right foot alternating between being on the accelerator pedal and off it – who asked me what I would do if a man of God surrendered to the lusts of the flesh in front of me at that very moment. I suggested that he discuss this with his bishop. The second was a wealthy semi-retired trucking magnate, who was greeted with familiarity in several bars and restaurants along our route. This evidently didn't extend to accommodation options, since at 2am he parked his car under a tree in a quiet French village and proceeded to strip off and bed down next to me. Fortunately, it had been such a long, wearying drive that he fell asleep after a few perfunctory and rapidly resisted gropes.

My allure had evidently diminished by the morning, and the journey settled into a less fractured rhythm. Dropped off by the disgruntled trucker outside a park in Lyon, I spent the following night under a bridge in Avignon on the banks of the Rhone – mandatory, having learnt the centuries-old French song "Sur Le Pont d'Avignon" at school – and continued south through a series of expediently lengthy rides that deposited me on a beach in Southern France one day and in Valencia the following night, with a few hours in Barcelona between. After that, it was a slow drive down the Mediterranean coast to Alicante where, emerging from a very long shower, I decided that I'd had enough. The novelty of repetitive conversations with helpful strangers along the way was losing its lustre, and I simply wanted to get home.

The cross-country train ride from Alicante to Seville took 24 hours, about twice the scheduled time, in midsummer temperatures. There were several breakdowns along the way. After a while, it didn't seem to matter when we arrived. Now, in an era of high-speed train travel where you receive a refund if your arrival is over five minutes late, the journey takes just six hours. If there were third-class carriages on this trip, I was travelling in one. It resembled the scene from films set in colonial India in which the last train is leaving a crowded conflict-torn area of the country with people hanging off the sides of the wagons. It wasn't just chickens in the compartment, it was an entire farmyard, a climate of unbelievable squalor, with a primitive toilet shared by over a hundred people becoming blocked after a few hours travel, then overflowing through necessary and continued use. When we finally reached our destination, all of us an entire day and night older and grubbier than we were when we boarded the train, we practically kissed the platform.

On the pier in Huelva, waiting for Puritano's boat to ferry us across the river to Corrales, my clothes a little the worse for wear and the beginnings of my first beard in evidence, I attracted some enquiring looks and partial recognition from my fellow travellers at the quayside, although none of the melodramatic horror at my new appearance that my mother would subsequently display. By this stage a bridge across the river had slowly begun construction and would forever change the landscape when it was completed and opened, eventually becoming part of a freeway linking Huelva and Punta Umbría, the idyllic village which once could be accessed from Huelva only by boat through the marshes.

There were now a few cars in Corrales, which immediately made it feel less isolated. Although it would be three more years until these were able to cross the river, they could now take a dirt track in the other direction through neighbouring Aljaraque to the coast at La Bota, and join the paved coastal road to Punta Umbría in one direction and Ayamonte, the border town with Portugal, in the other. Occasionally, we would hear about a traffic accident involving villagers, who had begun drinking at the few makeshift bars along the roadside and had then tried to drive home.

It was around this time that the feeling started – the awareness that I was no longer umbilically connected to the village, that having found some stabilising contentment at the end of my school years meant there was another version of life to be enjoyed, one less monopolised by a yearning for a time and place in the memory. During that exquisite summer, even as I was enjoying it, I increasingly sensed this withdrawal, I had a beautiful and companionable girlfriend, Mari Carmen, with whom I had gone to the *feria* in Seville earlier in the year and had returned from it a little intoxicated with her. She had grown up in the village, but had lived for some time in Barcelona, and was more worldly and playful than the other girls, whose lives as they grew up became more subsumed in parental custom. Mari Carmen had family in Seville too, and we travelled there and sweetly sweltered together through the hottest week of the Andalucian summer. She was quite wonderful, but as my own centre of gravity was shifting, so our relationship receded with it.

One day early in September, I boarded a mineral-carrying cargo ship – the kind I had once stood on the pier as a child and witnessed being loaded by cranes – which took us downriver to the ocean, made two right turns to follow the Atlantic coast of Portugal, rolled across the turbulent Bay of Biscay, and up through the English Channel to the Hook of Holland, from where I took a ferry to Harwich. On the subsequent train ride to London, someone in my compartment was playing a radio broadcast of songs from the Beatles' *Revolver* album, released a few weeks earlier. The ingenuity and imagination which had gone into honing its disparate elements into a completely integrated work was astonishing to me. This, and my subsequent discovery of the Beach Boys' *Pet Sounds*, further reinforced my belief, held to this day, that 1966 – in terms of ambition, innovation, melodic flair and lyrical adventurousness – was the finest year in history for recorded popular music.

I had a place at Birmingham University to study Spanish and Drama, so that was where I went. Although the most effective way to begin friendships and generate a social life at university was by staying in a hall of residence, having already spent half my life in boarding schools meant that this was not an attractive option for me. The other was to join a society that did more than just meet. Mine was the Guild Theatre Group. The stimulation and fulfilment of performing *The Zoo Story* in my penultimate term at school had given me an appetite for theatre, although at the core of this may have been a young man's yearning for the attention he was unable to attract in daily life. As a main subject, I had chosen one that would gain me entry and at which I could easily excel (Spanish), in order to explore one that truly interested me (Drama).

My first landlady, in the suburb of Kings Norton, was a lively, garrulous widow who, it became apparent, had really been seeking a young companion with whom to watch television in the evenings, a witness to her frequent commentary on the programmes being broadcast. As a lodger who was invariably at the cinema or a drama rehearsal at such times, I was a disappointment to her, and she was happy when I found other accommodation.

In my first couple of years in Birmingham, I directed and acted in two Spanish department plays (*Un Drama Nuevo* and *El Grillo*), appeared in the large Guild Theatre Group cast of Brecht's *Galileo* – which had us introducing the term "Brechtian" to every other sentence of our conversation during its run – and toured local schools with a trio of truncated highlights from Ann Jellicoe's *The Sport of My Mad Mother*, Arnold Wesker's *Roots* and Shakespeare's *Troilus and Cressida*, a triple bill perfectly of its moment. We saw this as an initiative in taking a range of thoughtful popular theatre to the people, but for the young students to whom we performed these plays, I suspect it was a wearying few hours, although they notably perked up and paid attention when a statuesque Chrissie Iddon, playing the central character Beattie Bryant in *Roots*, stood on a chair centre-stage in a mini-dress for her central soliloquy. There were some notable successes-to-be among fellow drama students of that period – director Barry Kyle, actors Tim Curry, Patrick Barlow, Judy Loe and Keith Drinkel, and writers Stephen Lowe and Alan Booth. In various combinations and settings, we also performed Ben Jonson's *Bartholomew Fair*, Wilde's *The Importance of Being Earnest*, six Cervantes short stories under the title *Speedy Gomez*, Marlowe's *Doctor Faustus*, and a new play by a fellow student Michael Walker called *Monkey*, set in a psychiatric hospital, which was a particularly extreme bonding exercise for those of us who acted in it. Everybody went off the rails in some way, particularly when we travelled together to Liverpool to present it there. After the show, we all drank several bottles of cheap cider and went into an intense huddle in our shared lodgings, listening repeatedly to a new album by the local poets' collective the Liverpool Scene, with Roger McGough's "Let Me Die a Young Man's Death", in particular, sending us all into an earnest and empathetic swoon.

The role I most wanted to play – but had to settle for a bus ride to Leicester to see it performed by someone else – was Jimmy Porter in John Osborne's *Look Back in Anger*. The play itself had not dated well in the intervening decade, dominated as it was by hectoring soliloquies from an angry, narcissistic protagonist who is always furious about something. However, what was invariably built into the best of such characters, beyond their vivid eloquence and emotional tightrope walking, was the potential for an actor to take them somewhere extraordinary. I believed that great playwrights (and, in his time, Osborne was one) were able to sense the shape and nature of the times, and to express these with energy and conviction and bold splashes of colour. I felt there was a suspicion, even a mistrust, of such intensity in the theatre of the late 60s, an underlying belief that characters who could express themselves with power and fluency somehow had less depth of feeling than the tentative and the inarticulate, who were reflexively deemed more authentic.

My interest in pop music, fuelled further by the comprehensive jukebox in the guild coffee bar, continued undiminished. My favourite location for listening to records – since I had no player of my own – was the upstairs library, where there were small sound-proofed listening booths. These had no ventilation, and you could smoke in them, creating a laboratory atmosphere in which the only available air was densely toxic, resembling those rooms you walked past in the transit areas of Asian airports in the early days of smoking bans, where the fog was so dense you couldn't see anyone inside. I would play wounded-loner songs such as Bob Lind's "Mr Zero", reflecting my now increasingly tiresome and alienating adopted self-image when what I yearned for most was a sense of belonging. Films, too, continued to fuel aspects of my behaviour. Just as Tarzan had once prompted me to swing between trees, so *Pierrot le Fou* made me want to smoke in the bath like Jean-Paul Belmondo and *Blow Up* to dress like David Hemmings.

Back in Corrales for my 20th birthday, I walked into a barbed wire fence. Some building works had begun in the mineral wasteland that was part of my route home, which in dim lighting and my dream state I did not acknowledge. Although erected to protect night wanderers like me from falling into a newly dug ditch, the wire itself was inexplicably at head height, so I was lucky not to lose both eyes. However, it did penetrate just above my upper lip, which was bleeding perceptibly. Surprised but still capable of thought, I realised that the recently arrived young village doctor Santiago and his Scandinavian fiancee Inger lived about a hundred metres away, and that they stayed up late, so I knew I could drop by for some unscheduled treatment, which was duly performed.

When I returned to Birmingham, I bought an old Hillman Minx for £35, and at weekends began driving down the motorway to London, visiting friends and sleeping on their sofas. Don Boyd – the only school friend I still knew with artistic leanings and a non-corporate career path – was starting a theatre group called Incognito to perform at the Edinburgh Festival Fringe and asked me to join it. Incognito had an entertaining and quite adventurous fringe repertoire – four plays, a mime show, improvisation sessions and a late-night review – which we rehearsed in London at weekends. I participated in a few things, but principally Ionesco's *The Lesson*, another one-act play that doesn't end well. This time I played a professor who murders his pupil.

The driving was constant, but there were bonuses within the boredom. Approaching Birmingham from the south on the return journey, as I now frequently did, I made an improbable but fascinating discovery which helped to assuage the repetitive tedium: after taking the freeway turn-off towards the city, the sound of the car tyres over this particular stretch of road surface emitted a kind of elongated whine of exactly the same frequency as the local accent.

On one of these rehearsal visits, I met Yoli, a late addition to the group, and an unignorable one in a green jumper. At the end of the evening, we took the same underground line in opposite directions and caught fleeting, smiling sight of each other as we simultaneously passed the corridor connecting our respective platforms. On such simple foundations are young romantic castles sometimes built, and the corresponding drawbridge opened.

We drove north together, first to Birmingham, where I packed up my flat and belongings, then continued the long haul to Edinburgh, extended by a couple of days as the blown gasket of my ancient car required rescue by a tow truck and enough time for a Lancashire village garage to locate a replacement. The dominant song of the trip was "Days" by the Kinks, whose wistful nostalgia was premature on one level but wholly anticipated on another, since soon after the Edinburgh Festival was over, I would be leaving for Spain to spend my third year of university in Madrid. Separation requires an acceptance of change, even an embrace of it, but for reasons to do with my own childhood I perceived it only as loss.

It was an idyllic time in Edinburgh, with whose geography and idiosyncrasies I was familiar from my school years. The company shared a large flat not far from where we performed, at St David's Church Hall in Viewforth. Except when either of us was on stage, Yoli and I spent every moment together, and in the early hours after the late show ended would pick up warm, fresh rolls from a bakery on the walk home and breakfast on them when we got there. There was no TV to distract us from each other, although BBC television had begun colour broadcasting, which could be watched through the display window of a nearby electrical goods store that thoughtfully kept a screen going after hours to attract new customers. There was a half-hour show called *Colour Me Pop* broadcast one evening, on which the Moody Blues appeared, reflecting the confusion of the times by performing a song called "Om" while resembling a quintet of Midlands hairdressers. And the Beatles' "Hey Jude" – a single whose seven-minutes-plus running time followed Richard Harris's comparably epic "MacArthur Park" earlier that summer – provided an exhilarating coda as we entered autumn and I prepared to leave the country.

In Madrid, it still felt like summer. Being one of the European capital cities furthest from the sea, it also appeared to retain heat the longest. Even a hint of breeze was elusive. I found a small apartment near the Plaza de Castilla, a simple journey on public transport from the city centre, and a short walk across a building site from the shiny prosperity of the Castellana's luxury hotels, if I wanted to dream a little. The walls were thin, and my next-door neighbours, whom I never saw, were audio-revealed to be a couple that simply couldn't understand each other. He was American, she Spanish. Neither spoke enough of the other's language to be comprehensible, so voices were raised as a matter of course, and no complete sentences were ever spoken. The air was dense with exasperation, their loudly declaratory break-ups and make-ups recurrent punctuation marks.

I checked in at the university, on a lush semi-rural campus in the western part of the city, which still appeared to be in some kind of seasonal limbo. Subsequent visits revealed little more, so

I concluded that the student unrest which had spread through Europe during the year had finally reached Madrid, despite there being no visible evidence of insurrection. Each time I went, there seemed to be decreasing numbers of people around, and I never found anyone to advise me on when and where to show up. I had assignments to complete during the year, so I concentrated on those instead, and was content to explore the city. *Madrileños* were struck by my accent, an impenetrable rustic Andaluz that took them by surprise. What they saw was an Anglo-looking young man who would likely elongate his Spanish vowels like foreigners did. What they *heard* was a field worker from the southwest with a crude peasant vocabulary. It was a disconcerting compound for them to accommodate. They were always looking, in vain, for the ventriloquist. And they still do.

After a few months, Yoli came from London to join me. I had already registered with a modelling agency and within days had my first photo shoot, wearing a tuxedo in a newspaper advertisement for Anis La Castellana. The others in the ad – a woman in the foreground, two men beside me and behind her – were French professional models who had flown in from Paris that morning. I had very thick dark hair resembling a sprayed-on helmet, and a perfect hippie moustache, so at least looked distinctive in the picture, and naturally the speed with which my first engagement had materialised encouraged me to believe that there might be a potential short-term career in it, certainly enough money to pay the rent.

With this in mind, Yoli and I both had modelling pictures taken and delivered them to whatever agencies would allow us in to discuss work possibilities. One of these was McCann Erickson, whose creative director Charlie Burlakov – a genial Armenian polyglot who spoke six languages – took us under his wing simply because he liked us. We didn't get any work out of it, but he and his wife Olga gave us something else – their friendship – and often invited us to dinner at their house with their friends and colleagues. Among the singularities of dining at Charlie and Olga's was that when the hard-working, early-rising hosts were ready to retire for the night, they did so unannounced, leaving their guests to stay for as long as they wished. At some point, we would realise that they were not returning to the table, acknowledge it, and continue the evening until everyone decided to go home. Luis Buñuel could not have scripted it more deftly.

Not far from their apartment was another house I had reason to visit on one endless and indelible night around this time. One evening, Yoli prepared dinner in our little kitchen, a tuna and rice dish we often had when we chose to eat at home. Soon after we finished, I began hiccuping. Half an hour later, the hiccups were becoming more frequent and emphatic. I thought that holding my breath might be an effective circuit-breaker for anything involving the chest, but regardless of how long I held it, the hiccups continued. By this stage, there was escalating pain to reinforce the internal unrest, and we tried various strategies to help settle it. Anything to break the cycle. I continued the controlled breathing. I walked around the apartment a dozen times, then around the block twice, then sat still. I did some floor exercises. Yoli tried her best to give me a fright – the folkloric remedy for my condition. I had a cold shower, then a warm shower. We had sex. We tried to sleep.

I had read somewhere that hiccups could have a fatal impact on the heart if allowed to go on too intensely for too long. Now, three hours later, this troubled me, and the pain was becoming more acute, like having intermittent thunderbolts in my chest. I was beginning to wonder if I needed a doctor or an exorcist.

Around 2am, I remembered once noticing a discreet gold plaque, advertising 24-hour medical consultations, on the door of a building about half an hour's walk away across the wasteland. My hiccups still raging, we dressed and set off. It was a cold night and we moved briskly. We approached the building, rang the doorbell, waited. The rustle of someone getting up, then a light coming on, the sound of slippers descending a staircase, and the outline of a figure in a dressing gown, perceptible through the frosted glass between the wrought iron panels. At that moment – the exact second the figure in the dressing gown opened the door – the hiccups stopped.

Although my own disconnection from Spain had been compounding over some time, the year in Madrid provided a completely satisfying closure – my first opportunity as an adult to live a continuous year in my native country since my departure to boarding school as a child, and my last opportunity, as it turned out, to spend any time there at all for nearly another decade. There was also the promise of a stable and contented personal life. I had taken Yoli south to introduce her to my mother and father in Corrales, and to spend Christmas with them. My parents had stopped paying any attention to Christmas after both their children had left home, so when Yoli and I wandered out into the countryside one afternoon and brought back a tiny pine tree which we decorated with some of their long-neglected seasonal trinkets, they were quite touched. By the time we went to visit them again in summer – both of us just 21 – it was to tell them we were getting married.

The bridge across the river to Huelva had finally been completed and opened. Growing numbers of people in the village now had televisions and cars. Tourists with blonde hair no longer attracted a crowd of onlookers. Corrales was ready for change – as was all of Spain, with Franco only six years away from death.

On our last night there – July 20, 1969 – we watched the Apollo moon landing on a village TV in a yard under a vividly starry sky. Everyone was spellbound, our comparative isolation intensifying the experience. The next day, we flew to London. There was a wedding to prepare.

CHAPTER FIVE

The wedding was at a church in Mayfair, the reception at the Royal Air Force Club in nearby Piccadilly. Yoli's father was a member, so I speculated that the arrangements had begun with the party venue and worked backwards from there. My mother and father were in Britain that summer – laying the foundations for retirement to the west of Scotland the following year – and my sister Lesley and cousin Christine attended as well. Between them and a couple of school friends, I felt solidly represented, if rather short on numbers. Everyone looked terrific except me, who in a three-piece black velvet suit with flared trousers resembled a store mannequin of the Swinging London era. Afterwards – a little dazed, perhaps even wondering what we had got ourselves into – Yoli and I spent the night at the Milestone Hotel, across the road from Kensington Palace, a likely base at the time for tabloid newspaper stakeouts of misbehaving young royals.

There was no honeymoon. We had already enjoyed one in advance, travelling around southern Spain and visiting Yoli's aunt in nearby Tangier, and we needed time to prepare a move to Birmingham to begin my final year at university. Shortly before leaving London, we discovered that Yoli was pregnant. Our excitement untainted by anxiety, we greeted the news without fuss, simply packing our clothes, renting a van and driving north. An early indication that fortune might indeed favour the brave was that we immediately found an idyllic little flat with a beautiful back garden, within close walking distance of the university and just across the road from the new maternity hospital we would soon be attending. If there was any latent concern about becoming parents at 21 – when we ourselves were still children – it was outweighed by the security we felt in each other, and by the harmonious environment we tried to build around us. Outside of university lectures – and writing and directing that year's Spanish department play, an adaptation of the 16th century novella *Lazarillo de Tormes* – it was a quiet life for a young student and his expectant wife. We had amicable neighbours, played constant music, took gentle walks, and sat in the garden, blissful in the bubble of our bucolic reverie.

When the time finally came, Yoli needed to have a Caesarian. Perceived to be unhelpful at such times, men were discouraged from being present at these deliveries, so from the final stages of labour my involvement was confined to repeated pacing of the waiting room, in which I remained completely alone during the entire process. When our son Jason had been born, and relief and delight been felt and declared and exhausted, I left the hospital, slept for a few hours, then did something highly irregular. I took the train to London to visit friends and to see Antonioni's *Zabriskie Point*, which had just opened exclusively at the giant Empire cinema in Leicester Square. (Remarkable as it now sounds, there is little I wouldn't have done at that time to see a film that really interested me. Once, as a schoolboy in transit at London's Heathrow Airport for a few hours, I discovered that Elvis Presley's *Jailhouse Rock* was playing an afternoon show in nearby Richmond, so I took a taxi outside the terminal, saw the film, and returned to the airport just in time for my connecting flight to Edinburgh.) Although my post-natal trip had been understood and agreed, it was undeniably an unexpected coda to an extraordinary event, even with the knowledge that Yoli's mother would be replacing me at her bedside during my time away. There were no conflicted feelings I can recall, no denial or dismissal – although almost certainly some delayed shock that I was now a father – but I felt oddly justified in wanting my own few days of recovery and adjustment, even if it was not me who had actually given birth.

I have many regrets about how I navigated the final year of my academic life. I simply didn't apply myself. I was lazy and dismissive, and I wasn't bright enough intellectually to get away with it. There was a good deal of anti-authoritarian posturing at the core of it, as there had been at school, but now cloaked in self-serving rationalisation. I would declare that true learning should not involve the artifice of exams, disregarding the fact that I wasn't doing much learning of any kind, just resentfully pontificating about it. Small acts of sabotage pointlessly punctuated my final exams. I answered one question by explaining why I didn't want to answer it, and why the education system itself was anachronistic. I was so entrenched in my self-satisfied hippie lair that I was unable to see the point of stepping out of it and making something serious and substantial of myself as a student. I received my degree anyway – probably in acknowledgement of the more committed work I had earlier delivered over the length of the course – but it was a perfunctory anti-climax to something that merited striving for more.

I was, however, a contented father. Nobody has any idea how young parenting is going to turn out – especially young parents themselves – but our son was a beautiful and buoyant baby. Although mothers and fathers are generally understood to be the custodians of small children, there were times when I felt that he looked after us – a little boy of such cheerful and resilient goodness that he was in some way protecting us, keeping us out of harm's way. He would wake up each morning bolt upright, a gummy grin declaring his pleasure at starting the day, defying us not to participate.

This feeling of wonderment was not shared by the landlords of the apartments we attempted to rent when we returned to London. Those who did not reject us on account of the baby invariably offered accommodation too confined to live in. We endured a week at 22 Hornton Street, Kensington, in a third-floor room filled to such an extent by our two unpacked trunks, mattress and cot that it left hardly any space for us. Our neighbour across the hall was a benign heroin addict, whose offer to entertain our baby boy in front of his permanently lit paraffin stove was all too easily declined. We lasted several months on the ground floor of 200 Holland Road, so close to the Shepherd's Bush roundabout that we could never open the window without inviting the prospect of carbon monoxide poisoning. The building had already been sold to a developer and was scheduled for demolition six months later, but we finally had a space that enabled us to unpack and settle, for a short time at least, on the perimeter of Central London. Although there was a room available in Yoli's family home in Ealing, I felt it important that we start our new life in London in a place of our own, and that we live close to where we thought we might find work.

Yoli made things and sold them at a shared stall in Kensington Market. I wanted to write about music and films. The first publication I visited was *Strange Days*, whose editor Mark Williams I had once met briefly when he lived across the road from me in Birmingham. Through events he promoted there, he had helped to convert Mothers, a small club in the suburb of Erdington, into a venue at which most of the adventurous bands of the period eventually played. Subsequently music editor of *International Times* – the foundation stone of London's underground press – he would later go on to establish and edit a motorcycle magazine called *Bike*, since he rode one. For now he was in the *Strange Days* office, being asked a scramble of overlapping questions by numerous functionaries trying to get the first issue of their magazine to the printers, and inviting me to submit reviews of whatever new records I felt like writing about. His assistant was an American girl called Corinne Schwab, who a couple of years later – by then always referred to as Coco – became David Bowie's assistant for the rest of his life. So I wrote a few pieces for them, mediocre fluff that for the most part accomplished little more than reflecting the way I wanted to project myself. It could only get better.

Strange Days did not survive for long, but I was now a published journalist of sorts, so I visited a magazine called *Friends* (later *Frendz*), whose offices were at the far end of the Portobello Road. There I got more work – and more records to review. Then I moved on to *Time Out*, located in a three-storey terrace at the Kings Cross end of Grays Inn Road. They also invited me to contribute editorially. These periodicals were different in emphasis and perspective, even in function, but fundamentally they were variations on an overlapping mix of news stories, arts profiles, counterculture politics, reviews, personal ads and, in the case of *Time Out*, listings of London events. All of them supported the legalisation of soft drugs – so accordingly were subjected to random police raids – and spoke directly to their readers. The most provocative of the publications – and therefore the one of which people were most aware – was *Oz* in Notting Hill Gate, the sybaritic lifestyles of whose editors, which appeared to involve boundless playful mischief, I envied profoundly. During my first full summer in London, the *Oz* obscenity trial, which filled the courts for two months in mid-1971, became the epicentre of conflict between generational attitudes. Life became increasingly about who you perceived yourself to be – and which side you wanted to be on. By then Yoli and I were back in Ealing with our baby – our bid for independence, for the moment, defeated – and I supplemented my modest writing income by working behind the counter in record shops in Queensway and Westbourne Grove, both mysteriously managed by people who knew absolutely nothing about contemporary music.

When the Rainbow Theatre opened in the hallucinatory Moorish splendour of the Finsbury Park Astoria in the autumn of 1971, *Time Out* was contracted to provide the design and editorial content for the theatre's free printed programme, which featured the bands performing at the venue during the relevant period. Our music editor would devote himself to writing and editing this programme, so over the time he was doing this he asked me to take over responsibility for *Time Out*'s own music coverage – event listings and record reviews – and to commission and contribute features. Unpractised in phone use, I now spent many hours collecting information through the one on my desk. Although earning a minimal salary, I was delighted – and a little nervous – to be where I was, around this unfamiliar abundance of opportunity, grateful that the enthusiasm and commitment that I had brought to my work on the magazine so far had compensated for my lack of sophistication and enabled me to settle into such a stimulating environment in my now adopted city. The day I began as a full-time staff member there, cherishing my sudden sense of belonging, I took the three floors of steps up to my little office under the roof two at a time.

The founder, publisher and editor of *Time Out* was Tony Elliott – the first of two remarkable employers I had in London over the following sixteen years who fundamentally ruined me for any future ones – a fearless, indefatigable, far-sighted maverick with a simple idea that revealed itself to be a great one: to create a magazine that satisfied the culturally curious contemporary Londoners whose desire to know their options were not represented by the fading, anachronistic *What's On*. This was a magazine he was sure people wanted, and he would deliver it to them fully formed, even if editorially its frantic publishing schedule sometimes made it vulnerable to typographical error. In its pages, Luis Buñuel's film *L'Age D'Or* was once famously retitled *Large Door*.

Time Out was both a source of event information and a publication about popular culture that considered politics to be a vital part of that culture. There was a sense of editorial freedom that couldn't be fabricated or bought, and the magazine covered most of the important issues of London life in its news pages – civil liberties, gay and women's rights, drugs, police corruption and so on. In the increasing factionalism and fragmentation of the counterculture, our offices were occasionally occupied by one disgruntled group or another: there would always be something to offend somebody. There was no office security in those days – the door was open and you could just walk in – although, to acknowledge that there was expensive equipment in the building, we did put on an alarm at night. I had never seen an alarm before and had only the slightest idea how it worked, but since I was frequently in the office late, I was instructed in how to set it. Once, on my own, I let it off soon after smoking a joint, which threw me into an unsettling panicky tailspin, an early indicator of how ill-suited I was to marijuana use. Then I would take the endless journey on the Piccadilly line to Ealing Common, across which I walked home each night for several weeks without ever seeing another person.

A side benefit of being employed by a high-profile magazine – the kind which rarely materialises when you aren't – is that people in adjacent fields begin to consider you employable by them as well. I was called one day by a Radio One producer, Jeff Griffin, and asked if I would contribute (and be paid more than my weekly salary for) a brief music news segment to a show which featured DJ Alan Black, a man I had listened to in my Loretto bedsitter study in very early 1966 when pirate Radio Scotland began broadcasting from outside territorial waters off the coast of nearby Dunbar. I was also sent records, invited to concerts and receptions, and encouraged to meet people I was interested in and interview them. This could be over a cup of tea at Abbey Road studios with Roy Harper, when he was recording the song "South Africa" for his album *Lifemask* – which, prompted by a recent diagnosis, he thought might be the last one he would survive long enough to complete. Or it might be an extraordinary five-hour career-spanning conversation with Kevin Ayers while together demolishing a bottle of whisky in a small Tottenham house shared with his Whole World band members, before unsteadily catching the last tube to Ealing. Or a bizarre afternoon in a basement near Baker Street talking to the guitarist Chris Spedding as his flatmates wandered around the room. Or an epic exchange with Pete Townshend of The Who, as much a virtuoso at making connections between ideas as he was about having the ideas in the first place.

My club and concert attendance was constant. I was insatiable, compensating for suppressed hunger with extreme greed. Clubs and concert halls can offer unpredictable experiences that records are unable to provide, and accordingly live music often generates surprises. One such event had an unexpectedly dramatic, potentially fatal climax, just as it appeared the show had already finished. At a Mothers of Invention concert at the Rainbow, Frank Zappa, completing a final encore with The Beatles "I Want To Hold Your Hand", was attacked by a member of the audience who – evidently deranged by his girlfriend's declared infatuation with Zappa, and by who knows what else – climbed on to the stage and pushed him into the ten-feet-deep concrete-floored orchestra pit. Zappa, whom the audience clearly thought might be dead, spent several months in a wheelchair after that and, it was said, narrowly escaped brain damage.

Continuing my transitory state of high employability, I was offered a job with *Rolling Stone*, whose plan was to generate more stories from their London office, pages of editorial for the magazine's British edition that might in turn attract more advertising. My move from *Time Out* to *Rolling Stone* was viewed by some with amused cynicism as social climbing in counter-cultural circles, and as an indication that in the underground press there was now such a thing as a career ladder, one on which I had just climbed a step. My reaction to this perceived promotion was an interesting one: I fell into an acute depressive trough. What I really yearned for, it turned out, was a holiday from everything, which I eventually took. My brief interlude at *Rolling Stone* was not productive, but there were a few highlights – a day spent with the group Caravan in a field outside Canterbury, and an office encounter with Suzi Quatro, whose recent recording of a song called "Rolling Stone" had evidently prompted her to visit our premises, escorted by her mother and still nearly a year away from her metamorphosis into the zippered, leather-jumpsuited rocker with a number 1 hit in "Can the Can".

I freelanced for a while, contributing regularly to both my former employers, *Time Out* and *Rolling Stone*, and to *New Musical Express* and several music monthlies. Some months earlier, while still at *Time Out*, I had written positive reviews of several records released by Dandelion, an unusually adventurous label founded by DJ John Peel and his manager Clive Selwood, both of whom wrote me courteous and appreciative postcards. An experienced record company executive when he wasn't being Peel's manager and friend, Selwood had recently joined CBS and invited me to do some copywriting for them at a time when the work was particularly welcome. Through this I met one of my heroes, Johnny Nash, whom I had once seen as a teenage actor in the film *Take a Giant Step* and who, as an adult singer – apart from his own hit records such as "I Can See Clearly Now" – was the first performer of note to popularise the songs of Bob Marley before Marley himself began to do so.

Peel was also somebody I had admired for some time, a compellingly low-key figure who resolutely ploughed his own field. On his Radio 1 programme *Top Gear* he played only music that interested him, which alone would make him a distinctive and significant figure in popular radio. His producer John Walters was an amusing, voluble, tireless raconteur who in some respects opened up Peel's world, making it looser, noisier, more varied, less virtuous, championing the ambitious, outlawing the pretentious. They had a close professional association, and were also good friends who went, with their wives, on a joint honeymoon. I can't remember which one of them described their relationship as "a bit like a master and his dog – each believing the other to be the dog", but it was unerringly exact. Peel once told a funny story about Walters' competitive nature, and the extremes of ingenuity to which he would go to ensure success.

At the time of the incident, their programme was broadcast on a Saturday afternoon. Afterwards they would drive down to Surrey together to spend the evening with their wives at the

Walters' house. BBC2 had introduced to their programming a late-night movie on a Saturday, and the parlour game was that each of them would take it in turn to prepare a meal consonant with the title or theme of that night's film, a meal they would unveil triumphantly to the others as the main credits rolled. Walters had previously shown himself to be quite inventive in this regard when at the beginning of the broadcast of the 1955 thriller *Footsteps in the Fog* he entered the room with a tray bearing four bowls of pea soup, a none-too-subtle reference to when dense London fogs were referred to as "pea soupers". On this particular Saturday night, *Foxhole in Cairo* – a film about, as Peel put it, "military unpleasantness in the desert" – was being shown, and again it was Walters' turn to serve the themed dinner. As the movie began, he brought in plates of curry. Peel groaned perceptibly at this, feeling that offering extremely hot food to accompany a film set in the desert was a little weak. But as they ate, the curry turned out to be very hot indeed, and glasses of water had not been offered. So, they went to the kitchen tap to alleviate their by now burning throats. No water emerged, because Walters had turned it off. Determined not to be defeated, they frantically climbed the stairs to the top of the house, where the tank was. Here was the final stroke of genius – Walters had emptied it, and had not eaten any curry himself.

Over a period, Yoli and I had become close friends with Kevin Ayers, his genial bass player Archie Legget, their respective girlfriends and their landlady – painter, poet and performer June Campbell Cramer, known to everyone as Lady June. June's convivial flat at Vale Court in Maida Vale was a magnet for interesting people – she and her lodgers were themselves manifestly that – and the location of numerous social gatherings, some spontaneous, others planned. The biggest of them all – and,

I expect, the last – was a birthday party in June 1973 at which Robert Wyatt, by then also a friend, drunkenly locked himself in the bathroom with a young woman, and when his girlfriend (later wife) Alfie began banging on the door decided to climb out the window rather than face her fury. Several floors up, and with no conveniently located drainpipe, he fell a long way to the ground, broke his back and became paralysed from the waist down. First out of the door and the building as the news rapidly circulated was the most famous person present, a man well into his period of heroin addiction who was clearly trained to disappear with reflexive speed from any place in which the police might take an interest – Keith Richards.

We visited Robert some weeks later in the spinal injuries centre of Stoke Mandeville hospital near Aylesbury, where Alfie's friend Julie Christie sat quietly by his bedside reading a book while preparations were under way for a house she owned in Twickenham to be adjusted to Robert's needs when he was eventually discharged from the hospital. Despite his life-changing injuries and the circumstances that would inevitably follow, he was as philosophical and as good-natured as ever, his modesty and valour eclipsing the rage and self-pity he would have been justified in feeling.

Robert and Kevin had been in the group Soft Machine with Mike Ratledge, who was still in it. He was the last founder member of what was by then a musical entity whose shape shifted in accordance with its changing personnel. Their album titles had all been numbers, and at this point (*Seven*) no two successive LPs had featured exactly the same core musicians. I knew Mike a little, and admired him intellectually – a formidably articulate and iconoclastic interview with him had appeared in a 1969 issue of *Oz* – but it was with the group's manager Sean Murphy that I sometimes drove to see them at out-of-town concerts. Sean called me one morning to ask if we could meet to talk. It turned out that WEA (Warner-Elektra-Atlantic), a mighty confluence of American music companies, was starting a "boutique" label for UK acts, and that he had been asked to run it. Would I join him, he asked. I decided I would.

CHAPTER SIX

Our premises at 69 New Oxford Street were palatial to me, who had only been an occasional visitor to such environments since arriving in London. Still, if WEA was a giant ocean liner Raft was indeed a raft, although not an uncomfortable one. On it were Sean Murphy, Mark Rye (who did radio and TV promotion), Tony Gourvish and me. Tony was the manager of three of the four acts signed to Raft – the newly-dissolved Family, their successors Chapman-Whitney Streetwalkers and singer Linda Lewis. Understandably, given his history with the company and its artists, he considered himself highly qualified to run it. WEA may have thought him overqualified in the wrong way, a combustible cocktail of conflicting interests, so had not offered him the job. The first time we'd met was when I interviewed him at his flat in Knightsbridge, where I arrived early one morning just as Caroline Coon – who founded and ran the well-known 24-hour drug and legal advice centre, Release – was leaving. The second was when collecting something from him at a house in Notting Hill, and Germaine Greer opened the door in a dressing gown. Evidently he had a taste for clever, combative, high-profile women, and they for him. He was immediately energising company, bouncing into our office several times a day with promotional ideas for his artists as he was devising them.

My job was to get our acts written about in the press. For me it was also a matter of by whom and in what manner. It is difficult to understand from today's perspective the tremendous importance of the four music weeklies (*Melody Maker, New Musical*

Express, Sounds and *Record Mirror*), which together sold hundreds of thousands of copies each week, in establishing a presence, familiarity and status within the British music scene. For several years I had read every music periodical from cover to cover – even when living in Madrid, where they were obtainable at only one location in the city – so I knew the tastes of all the writers (without having yet met them), had a feel for which journalist to approach with each artist and could determine who would be the most effective interviewer for what individual. It was a confluence of honed instinct and researched pragmatism, and Raft, with its small roster built on what appeared to be the stable foundations of a substantial empire, was the perfect place to learn how to do the job without the inhibiting weight of excessive responsibility.

I made a few errors of etiquette by mistakenly following common sense instead. One was to invite journalists for a drink at a pub across the road from the Marquee club in Wardour Street, instead of at the bar of the Marquee itself, where Beckett – our fourth act, a Newcastle band yet to record their first album – were later playing. This caused some discontent in the club's management, who seemed unwilling to understand the folly of arranging a social gathering in a place where the music was too loud for us to hear each other speak. With my few colleagues I felt very much at ease, as I also did with the equally few artists. One weekend morning, I took my son Jason, not yet four, to Linda Lewis's flat in Chiswick, where Linda and her boyfriend/producer Jim Cregan (who had been in the final incarnation of Family and was soon to join Rod Stewart's band) entertained him with great warmth. Roger Chapman and Charlie Whitney – whom I first saw with Family in 1968, an aerial view from the very top of the Albert Hall, the only ticket I could afford – were recording with their new group, and Yoli and I often visited Sean, Mark and

Tony and their respective partners. Tony was by then courting the model Jane Lumb, whom he would go on to marry. The only new band we signed during this period was Kilburn and the High Roads, whose immense entertainment value on stage would prove more elusive to capture in the recording studio, where they were working on an album that Raft did not survive long enough to release. They had an extraordinary singer and songwriter in Ian Dury, a kind of cockney Cole Porter whose ingenuity with lyrics, and indelible way of delivering them, made him a unique presence in the contemporary music of the time. His day would surely come, as it did a few years later, with his next group The Blockheads.

As 1974 dawned, British prime minister Edward Heath's government's response to the world's oil shortage, Britain's anticipated energy crisis, and the industrial unrest that was unfolding all over the country, was to declare a three-day working week in the UK throughout January and February. This made little difference to our own work, which continued as usual, but the manufacturing of vinyl discs was unavoidably affected, requiring WEA's record pressings to come from its more energy-abundant European satellites, with correspondingly higher costs. Although this would have engendered economic caution in our owners, it nevertheless came as a surprise when they suddenly closed us down. WEA SINKS RAFT was the not unexpected headline in the trade weekly *Music Week*. There were instructions from America, they declared, that they should concentrate exclusively on building the Warner, Elektra and Atlantic labels in the UK – which was, after all, why the umbrella company was called WEA – and not on us, a dollar-consuming distraction. I wrote and circulated my own self-righteous press release on behalf of Raft, outlining our virtues and achievements. "it was the executioners, rather than the victims, who were blindfolded", it concluded. I was offered a job by Atlantic, which I declined, because although the bacchanalian twilight zone one reputedly entered as a mandatory part of touring with their top British act Led Zeppelin would undoubtedly have opened up my world, I was still working out my own way of doing things and didn't want to be taking orders from American bosses, or from the group's famously disagreeable manager Peter Grant.

Then there was a phone call from Richard Branson. I invariably try to establish one detail about the people I meet which reveals them in some unusual way, and so provides a simple code to who they are. I was obviously aware of the record mail order company he had started, and the retail shops which followed, but as an early purchaser of *Student* magazine, which he had founded and edited, I'd heard a story that he had once shown up to interview the great American writer James Baldwin for the magazine without having read any of his books, and without Baldwin being aware of it during their conversation. (Richard later assured me that he *had* read the books.) This, I felt, is what defined him: his brazen, unparalleled chutzpah. I had met him a year earlier when he'd invited me to his houseboat at Little Venice to have dinner and listen to the first record Virgin was about to release, Mike Oldfield's *Tubular Bells*. His wife Kristen was present, as was Simon Draper, who was in charge of the new label. We duly dined and listened, and a couple of weeks later I wrote about it for *NME*, as everybody called *New Musical Express*. It was a positive review, reflecting my admiration for what Oldfield had been able to achieve, which was to amalgamate familiar musical sounds in a completely surprising way, re-contextualising them in the process and creating an unexpected work of popular art. After John Peel played the entire record on his radio programme one night, it combusted into a life of its own and was now approaching its first anniversary. On the back of it and Tangerine Dream's *Phaedra* album, Virgin had cruised through a successful first year of business as a record company when sales of their other discs had been modest and there had been no hit single to keep cashflow buoyant.

During the call, Richard asked me if I would visit him in his office at the end of the working day, and I did, strolling down Portobello Road from Notting Hill Gate until I reached an alley just past the intersection with Westbourne Grove. It was late and everybody else appeared to have gone home. By then, at Kristen's insistence, he had bought a house a few minutes walk from the office, while the houseboat he already owned gradually became his centre of operations, a place where he could receive people more discreetly, somewhere they didn't have to walk past his entire staff to reach his office.

There really wasn't much to discuss. I was familiar with all the Virgin acts, felt I understood what made each of them who they were, and could anticipate where the right kind of publicity might take them, but I made it clear that I wouldn't work for less than I was being paid at Raft. This turned out to be more than anyone else at Virgin was earning, so he asked me to leave his office for a moment while he talked on the phone to his business partner, Nik Powell. A few minutes later, I walked out ready to start work in two weeks, an appointment which led to my first mention in *Melody Maker*'s "Raver's Hot Licks" column as "the only PR we know who can speak in complete sentences". This immediately felt like a distinction of sorts.

The music business did not have much regard for precision of language, although I felt I had found an improbable ally in Bryan Ferry when he released his second solo album *Another Time,*

Another Place that summer. Its title had not yet been announced when Ferry was asked by a reporter what it was. *"Another Time Comma Another Place"*, he replied, which was the way the title appeared in the headline of the report. I silently applauded his fastidiousness.

I had also started being invited to occasions with which I had no connection beyond fleeting familiarity; to John Peel's wedding reception in the garden of a Regent's Park house, where Rod Stewart, in mid-remodel from local lad to transatlantic rock star, was the preeminent guest; to the village of Woburn to play cricket for Roy Harper's XI against Pink Floyd's; to Floyd manager Steve O'Rourke's house in Esher, where I swam in a heated outdoor pool for the first time as snowflakes fell on my head and shoulders. This was the life.

I began at Virgin on June 3 1974, chronic flu nullifying my first day in the office, which looked even more primitive when you filled the empty spaces of my previous visit with people. It was a galaxy away from WEA, the staff toilet a single cubicle opening directly into the press and promotions office, whose corridor status made privacy impossible to achieve. I installed a perspex screen around my desk area to enable me to maintain focus in introductory conversations with all the label's artists and avoid turning these into broadcasts to the passing foot traffic. Most of the Virgin acts were quite restricted in their appeal, but they were adventurous and driven and populated by extremely bright people who brought intellectual acuity, as well as musical conviction, to what they did – Henry Cow, Hatfield and the North, Slapp Happy, Kevin Coyne, and so on. Each had their idiosyncrasies and a couple of the bands (Henry Cow and Slapp Happy) even amalgamated for two albums, with each playing on the other's record before the inevitable collisions of style and ideology divided and fractured them. As people, I was particularly intrigued by Peter Blegvad and Anthony Moore of Slapp Happy, who gave a highly discursive interview to *NME*, questioning the point of such interviews and the meaningless compromise required from both parties, a stream of consciousness which the paper chose to run practically unedited. Although quite different personalities, they were compatible spirits – articulate, argumentative absurdists, incapable of prompting or participating in a dull moment. Hatfield and the North, in contrast to their serious musicianly image, were playful and amusing. I rarely missed an opportunity to see them perform, and even made an appearance at their concert at the Collegiate Theatre, playing a nauseating holiday camp compere who introduces the members of the band towards the end, my first stage appearance since the 1968 Edinburgh Festival Fringe. From all accounts, it was a disturbingly convincing performance.

The immediate priority, however, was Mike Oldfield – because of the imminent release of *Hergest Ridge*, the successor a year later to the stratospherically successful *Tubular Bells*, and also, more surprisingly, by the issuing of a belated *Tubular Bells* single. If it weren't unusual in itself that an epic piece as integrated as *Tubular Bells* could be edited satisfactorily to single length, as it had been, its striking use by director William Friedkin on the soundtrack of his film *The Exorcist* prompted Richard to believe that, while *Tubular Bells* itself was well known, Oldfield's name was not. So he wanted the single to be titled "Mike Oldfield's Single" – with a reference to TB confined to parentheses – so that any time somebody was ordering the record they would have to say his name. It worked – as did *Hergest Ridge* which, despite muted reviews, went straight to the top of the album sales chart in the same week that its predecessor was in second position. This was extraordinary, particularly for a new record company, and the fact that neither record included any hit songs that might help propel sales, was a further distinction.

My good fortune in landing at Virgin at this moment in its evolution was further reinforced by Robert Wyatt. Since emerging from hospital and rehabilitation, he and Alfie had moved into their new home in Twickenham, and he had been recording with his friend Nick Mason, who with Pink Floyd had participated in two fund-raising concerts for him. I had high hopes for the album that would emerge from these sessions – the first he had done since the two Matching Mole albums before his accident – but *Rock Bottom* eclipsed them all: a fractured, dreamy, hallucinatory song cycle that cast a spell and engulfed you. When they'd finished it, they had also, to our surprise, recorded a version of Neil Diamond's "I'm a Believer", once a hit for The Monkees, to which Robert's poignant vocal brought an unexpected emotional sting. It was irresistible. We couldn't stop listening to it in the office, and daytime radio play – which Virgin could rarely count on – soon followed. It was high summer, and on one of a succession of cloudless days Robert and Alfie had a beautiful wedding party in their back garden. He was very much back in the world.

When "I'm a Believer" entered the Top 30, the BBC television programme *Top of the Pops* came calling. We were delighted, since an appearance on this was mandatory for a single's chances of further success. Our assumption was that Robert would perform the song from his wheelchair, so when the producer of the show told us that their viewers would find this too confronting on a light entertainment show and that they wanted him to sit in an armchair, we refused on his behalf. They threatened to withdraw the invitation. We insisted that they honour it. And so Robert became the first – and, for the three decades that the weekly programme subsequently continued to broadcast, the only – performer to have delivered their hit song from a wheelchair. As a sting in the tale, when he was preparing for his first concert at the Theatre Royal Drury Lane, he and his fellow musicians all sat in wheelchairs for an *NME* cover photo – part ironic postscript, part declaration of solidarity.

His support act at Drury Lane was Ivor Cutler, a writer, poet and former teacher I had once interviewed when he and his equally uncategorisable fellow Scot Ron Geesin appeared, separately, at a Soft Machine concert in Croydon. Ivor and Ron were both completely distinctive artists, each operating in a field of one. Ron was also a fine arranger (Pink Floyd's *Atom Heart Mother*, Bridget St John's *Songs for the Gentle Man*), and Ivor went on to make three records for Virgin – just him and his harmonium, with occasional punctuation from his partner Phyllis King. None of these sold many copies, but they were cheap to record and in some respects epitomised the kind of low-budget singularity on which Virgin was founded and which the success of *Tubular Bells* still made affordable. He was also an engaging lunch companion who had no interest in record business chatter. At the now long-gone Bertorelli restaurant in Queensway, we would see where the conversation took us, and when it was over he would give me a parting gift of his latest small gold-coloured rectangular labels, on which he would have printed an amusing maxim that he thought merited attention.

Like Mike Oldfield, Tangerine Dream – some of us nicknamed them "the Tangs" to lighten their perceived gravity – had also been a crucial asset to the survival and well-being of Virgin, and their cathedral concerts (Reims, Liverpool, Coventry, York Minster) had emancipated the group's electronic music from the restrictions of concert venues and helped give it the transcendent scale it merited, The group's Coventry Cathedral concert was filmed by the director Tony Palmer, who lived near our office in a house with its own editing room, and who would later use all of *Tubular Bells* over NASA footage in his film *The Space Movie*, which in 1979 commemorated the tenth anniversary of the moon landing. From another house near our office – Richard's own – would occasionally come a request to meet at some improbable hour. When Tangerine Dream's live album *Ricochet* was ready for release and its cover art nearly finalised, Yoli and I received a call from him one Sunday evening, asking us over to comment on the sleeve design, which was troubling him. It was laid out on the floor next to him, and as we spoke, he wrote down everything we said. Then he picked up the phone, called the group's leader Edgar Froese and paraphrased our observations without missing a beat.

Although Virgin championed artistic endeavour, it was the commercial performance by at least some of its contracted artists which enabled us to pay for this, so we were not above the occasional old-fashioned publicity stunt to get attention and, we hoped, sales. These rarely worked for us. When Anthony Moore released his single "Johnny's Dead" (credited to "Slapp Happy featuring Anthony Moore", despite the fact that the group no longer existed and its other members did not participate), we publicised it with a funeral procession around the local streets, with a horse-drawn hearse and a handful of mourners in dark clothing. The unanticipated element was that when the day came it was the hottest of the summer. Anthony was a sufficiently good sport to lie still in a coffin with his eyes closed and be dragged around the neighbourhood until heat fatigue kicked in and everybody went home. (Anthony's subsequent album, *Out*, was recorded but not released, and so was routinely referred to as *Not Out*. Finally disinterred by another record label over a decade later, it had aged well and regained its rightful title.) On another occasion, when Mike Oldfield had recorded the "William Tell Overture" as a stand-alone single and was living reclusively in the Gloucestershire countryside, I thought it might help its chances of being a hit if a reporter and photographer from the highest-circulation UK daily the *Sun* travelled to his house with the glamorous model Stephanie Marrian (who had already appeared on a Virgin album cover with a boxing glove positioned over her pubic hair), and that a picture be taken in which popular music's quietest man was about to fire an arrow at an apple on top of her head. As an unlikely collision of show business archetypes, what more could anyone want? When we finally arrived after the long drive from London, Mike's large dog went straight up to Stephanie, buried its head enthusiastically between her legs and practically lifted her right off the ground. By the end of the visit, Mike could hardly wait to get rid of us. The record was not a hit.

We continued to expand into other interesting musical territory – from distributing the great European jazz label ECM in the UK to signing such prominent reggae acts such as U-Roy, the Mighty Diamonds and Peter Tosh, attracting a wave of purist policing with regard to the possible "rockification" of roots reggae. My response was that we viewed it *all* as popular music, that if we didn't treat the music we liked as popular nobody else would, and that while we intended to popularise our Jamaican artists, they were under no commercial pressure to do anything they didn't want, since they simply sent us finished masters for release. This suspicion and concern was prompted by the expanding welcome being afforded to what had once been regarded, in mainstream circles, as ethnic esoterica. Reggae was now an undeniable force, but a divisive one. When U-Roy and the Mighty Diamonds appeared sequentially at the 1976 Reading Festival, beer cans flew between the people who were hostile to reggae and began throwing them as missiles, and those enjoying the show, who threw them right back. It was a disturbing and dangerous scene, particularly when the cans were full. We had also signed the remarkable and enduring German group Can (who had a surprise mini-hit with "I Want More") and the tirelessly entertaining Liverpool band Supercharge, who not only supported Queen at an enormous free concert in Hyde Park, but were later among the first groups to perform at the legendary club Amnesia in Ibiza, although they had the misfortune of playing at midnight in a venue that peaked at dawn.

I had a freedom at Virgin that I cherished, and of which I became particularly aware when I met counterparts at other record companies who were unable to do their jobs with the kind of unbridled spontaneity I was never denied. We never employed outside publicists. If I wanted to make fun of corporate self-importance by inventing a ridiculous new title for myself (or others) I could. I was also able to write outraged letters to periodicals without consultation, argue with journalists over errors or omissions they made in print, and push media relations to the limit while never losing control. We even had a soccer team – which played on a ground behind Wormwood Scrubs jail – and there was a squash club around the corner where I could exercise (and exorcise) away a difficult morning with a lunchtime game. Although aware that sport has always been the great equaliser of society across the ages, it was nevertheless strange to be standing naked in the showers afterwards next to Spike Milligan, a comedy idol from adolescence who turned out to be as entertaining nude as he was fully clothed.

An additional benefit of the flexibility I enjoyed was being able to put together compilation albums of people who interested me but recorded for other record companies. I compiled, sequenced and annotated three of these for the EMI label Harvest. One was a collection of unreleased tracks and obscure or deleted singles by Kevin Ayers I called *Odd Ditties* – odd, as in collected together for the first time, and odd also as in idiosyncratic, bizarre, curious, funny. There were also comprehensive career histories of Roy Wood and of Soft Machine, which took a little longer. With Soft Machine, I planned a triple album (to be titled *Triple Echo*), a chronological history of group recordings over a nine-year period, reflecting each stage of their development, not simply a compendium of personal preferences. My attempt to bring together its key members for a conversational reunion at Robert Wyatt's house in Twickenham to discuss its contents began well but ended badly, so I was left to my own devices in assembling it. Simpler (and for Virgin) was Mike Oldfield's four-disc *Boxed* – each of his three albums re-mixed in quadraphonic sound, plus a record of entertaining one-offs called *Collaborations*.

One of his collaborators on these was David Bedford, who had known him since playing together in Kevin Ayers' group The Whole World. David was a composer of modern classical music, and the singing teacher at a posh girls' school, Queen's College in Harley Street. He had arranged and recorded a version of *Tubular Bells* with the Royal Philharmonic Orchestra with Mike playing guitar, which had been performed live on several occasions with other guitarists – Steve Hillage and Andy Summers, among them – standing in for Mike, who avoided stage appearances during this period. David had also made three ambitious solo albums for Virgin in successive years, and in many ways represented the problem the label was beginning to face. There was an undeniable congestion in the air. We were releasing too many records and had accumulated more artists than we could support, remaining loyal to those we admired even when their sales were steadily diminishing, and we had not recently had the compensation of a new breakthrough by anyone. A year earlier, Richard and Simon Draper had been keen for us to sign a major band for however much money could be raised from our licensees to secure them – the Rolling Stones and 10cc were both close calls in this regard. Now, a number of contracts – among them, David Bedford's and Ivor Cutler's – were coming up for renewal, and the company had to choose what path to take and with whom in our attempt to put ourselves back on course.

When Richard called a staff meeting at his house to discuss and decide this, some thought it might be another of his practical jokes, which were the stuff of legend. Earlier in the year, he had taken two of his employees, who lived together, for dinner at Semiramis, a tiny Greek restaurant in Bayswater which we all frequented and sometimes filled entirely. While they were enjoying a long evening together, the crew of a large removals truck had been given a duplicate key to the couple's flat and had systematically stripped the place of absolutely everything. The couple returned home at around midnight to a completely empty apartment. Even their bed had gone. In a brilliantly reflexive act of revenge, they quickly reciprocated by calling the police, identifying Richard as the perpetrator, and having him arrested and put in a holding cell until halfway through the following morning – which was April Fools Day.

Ours was instead a long, complex and quarrelsome night, because we were all fundamentally admirers of the very people we were about to set adrift to float on the unreliable buoyancy of market forces. Naturally, I argued the most forcefully for retaining

Ivor Cutler, but I had to acknowledge that, although his records were inexpensive to make, there were unavoidable and undeniable costs in pressing, marketing and promoting them, and that in talking about the long-term survival and prosperity of the company, we were also all arm-wrestling over a pit of scorpions, reluctant to drop anyone in it. Only with Kevin Coyne was there unanimity of support to retain him.

When informed of the decision not to renew his contract, David Bedford wrote two letters – one to Richard Branson, declaring that he was sad but accepted the decision, observing that he'd had much support from Virgin, acknowledging that his records had not performed commercially, and realising why we were calling a halt. The other was to Mike Oldfield to say Virgin were a bunch of philistines who didn't know a crotchet from a quaver, and that it was typical of our cynical opportunism that we had dumped him. He put each letter in the wrong envelope, and mailed them. So Richard received the Dear Mike letter, and Mike the Dear Richard letter. On receipt, they called each other and exchanged.

We had been too busy ploughing our own field to notice the changing landscape around us. We had done so conscientiously, adventurously and, for the most part, effectively, but now the world was accelerating and we needed to keep up. Something was about to come into our lives that would both shake and strengthen our foundations.

CHAPTER SEVEN

During the second half of 1976, the incoming tide of punk became unavoidable, washing over and waking up the sleeping custodians of popular culture. It emerged from an unanticipated but expedient collusion between something fresh happening in popular music – the defiance of the reigning rock technocracy – and the pragmatic needs of a music press that hadn't had anything new to write about in years.

Although espousing individual expression, punk had a highly identifiable and regimented aesthetic – stripped-down, functional, edgy, confronting – that characterised its art, fashions, music, clubs, and attitude, particularly attitude, which was crucial, with a pulse beat perceptibly more skinhead than hippie. Speed was the primary drug of choice, aggression the social weapon of preference. The old-guard bands and executives, for so long accustomed to ruling the pop kingdom, some of them barely out of their 20s, found themselves prematurely middle-aged and out of touch, anxious to appear cool and compliant while in reality vulnerable and uncertain about their diminished status within a changing world they hadn't anticipated. Where they had once swaggered with entitlement, they were now targeted for hostility and ridicule, even if most of it was verbal. When they began visiting punk venues like anthropologists, they didn't come alone, huddled together as if on a life raft, fearful of a sudden shark attack.

The crown princes of this mutating universe were the Sex Pistols who, under the relentless navigation of their manager Malcolm McLaren, had succeeded in signing a contract with

EMI Records, recording a single ("Anarchy in the UK"), being dismissed from the label over their disorderly behaviour on a television interview programme (but pocketing the substantial cash advance without having to deliver any more recordings), signing a second agreement with A&M – photographed in a stunt at the roundabout outside Buckingham Palace as their limo circled it – only to be fired by them too (more allegations of thuggish conduct, this time in the company's offices afterwards), again retaining the advance. Derek Green, who was running A&M at the time, told of taking a day off work following the signing and driving to Brighton, where he sat on the beach contemplating if he could tolerate a life which involved the Sex Pistols and the reign of terror he anticipated would come with them. He couldn't, and when he returned to London he didn't. So within a few months, two major record labels had contracted, paid advances to, and then jettisoned the group. McLaren – a clothes shop owner and agitator, who viewed himself as a revolutionary with a disruptive Situationist perspective on anti-social behaviour – could hardly believe his confluence of luck, timing and strategy. Behave badly, get fired, keep the money – practically a t-shirt slogan. "The whole notion of the Sex Pistols", he later declared in a magazine interview, "was to be totally irresponsible and struggle for immortality".

Sometime between the EMI and A&M episodes, the group had dumped their bass player Glen Matlock – among the ru-moured reasons, for the heresy of liking the Beatles and, worse, admitting it. His replacement Sid Vicious was not known to play bass guitar, or any other instrument, but he had an abundance of aggression and attitude, and he increasingly enjoyed throwing his weight around in a way that reflected his nickname. I had first encountered him some time before he joined the Pistols, on a coach trip back from the 1976 Reading Festival, when we stopped the bus by the side of a country road to enable some of the passengers to relieve themselves of the ocean of beer they had put away while watching the bands play. Sid took about ten minutes to empty his bladder, prompting disbelief as he was doing it and mass applause when he finally and triumphantly climbed back on board.

They may have been looking for a third walk-away cash advance from us, but instead found a company which at that moment was seeking some mischief for its own reasons, and whose sense of risk, iconoclasm and adventure was complementary to theirs. Virgin had always been a little irregular within the record business, invariably following its own tastes and championing all kinds of ambitious music during its few years of existence. But what it hadn't accomplished since *Tubular Bells* was to apply its self-confidence, and its appetite for playful and provocative exploitation, to the reinforcement of a phenomenon, which the Sex Pistols might clearly be. For the company, it was the adrenalised shot in the arm that opened the door to the remarkable decade of success which followed. For me personally, it was as if someone had detonated a bomb, and my job was to walk calmly in silent slow-motion through the consequent falling debris.

The first thing was not to be intimidated by what we had now helped to set in motion. The second was to release the group's new single "God Save the Queen" one week before the Queen's Silver Jubilee, which was to be celebrated, with bunting and street parties as far as the eye could see, on June 7 1977. Immediately, there was a ban on its broadcast by BBC TV and radio, by the IBA (Independent Broadcasting Authority), the overseer of all commercial radio stations – despite the record already being on the playlists of individual stations – and by nationwide chain stores such as WH Smith and Boots. This notwithstanding, the record was selling over 20,000 copies a day, confirming that the assumed power of broadcasters could be eclipsed by curiosity and public interest.

The reaction was astonishing, and because I dealt with all aspects of Virgin's public relations, I found myself obliged to make statements constantly, which I tried to do without either militancy or capitulation, settling on a kind of deadpan directness. I mentioned that if the BBC's main objection to the song was the use of the term "fascist regime" (rhyming with "Queen"), and the country wasn't one, a fundamental principle of democracy would surely be for the national broadcaster to allow the song to be broadcast. It was certainly curious at a time when Britain was flaunting its freedom of expression that the most popular record in the country should be banned simply for not falling into line with Jubilee sentiments. And the fact that this record was likely to be in the top position of the BBC-sponsored British Market Research Bureau chart was a problem the BBC itself might need to resolve. I predicted that it would lead to egg on faces in high places. As it turned out, it didn't, because it was placed second, with Rod Stewart's "I Don't Want to Talk About It" – which we subsequently discovered had sold fewer copies than "God Save the Queen" – at No. 1. It all had the unmistakable whiff of expediency, collusion and self-interest.

By then, we had organised one of the most unusual concerts in popular music history, probably the shortest, and certainly the most comprehensively chronicled by the relatively few people who attended. The idea came from Malcolm McLaren, who was still testing Virgin's nerve for high-wire stunts. To his surprise, we endorsed it enthusiastically, and set about making it happen. The Pistols would play some songs – including their two best-known fire-starters, "Anarchy in the UK" and "God Save the

Queen" – from a boat on the Thames as it passed the Houses of Parliament. In effect, they would be performing confrontational anthems of insurrection outside the headquarters of government. Someone duly went to Charing Cross pier, approached the captain of a modest party boat and made a booking, explaining that a German synthesiser group would be giving a small concert on board for selected guests on Jubilee Day. Everything apart from the German synthesiser group was true. I was going to phone a few journalists I thought might enjoy the cruise, but they called me instead, such was the speed at which this kind of information travelled even in that era.

Once a boat leaves a jetty anything can happen, particularly when a photograph of the Queen with a safety pin through her nose is by then decorating the vessel. Despite a closely controlled guest list – numerous people were declined or left behind – we were still a lively and substantial group, first heading eastwards beyond Tower Bridge – waved to by someone dressed up as the Queen from the balcony of a Bermondsey warehouse – then turning around and cruising back upriver towards Westminster Bridge and Parliament. The group began to play and had been doing so for a few minutes as we approached the House. It was at this point that we attracted the attention of the river police, who began following us as the music continued, instructing the captain by loudspeaker to return to the pier, and escorting us all the way to it. There we were charged with public nuisance, disturbing the peace, and as many other offences as they could invoke on the spot. Richard Branson was emphatic with the police about us being completely within our rights, but McLaren, immediately combative, went further. He practically defied them not to arrest him, which they duly did. At Bow Street police station, things didn't calm down for some time. It remains an occasion which lingers in the folkloric memory of the music business because, in an industry which constantly craves attention, there was never another occasion quite like it.

By this stage, McLaren had become so intoxicated with ideas of profitability through conflict that he viewed our willingness to collude with him with great suspicion, perhaps because we were never overawed by him and consistently supported and defended the group. The sense of drama around them continued to escalate when two weeks later John Lydon (whose Pistols moniker Johnny Rotten would endure only as long as the group did), drummer Paul Cook and the Sex Pistols' art director Jamie Reid, were each attacked by gangs of men armed with knives or iron bars in different areas of London over a few days. All were hospitalised, Rotten and Cook requiring stitches, and Reid the resetting of a broken nose and a cracked bone in his leg. It was beginning to feel as if a war was under way, a national hatred, an open season on vigilantism. For a time, they stopped talking to the press, so the press instead called me, constantly. I attempted to answer each enquiry individually rather than issue statements. Although this was time consuming, it ensured that we were usually given an opportunity to comment on, and correct, misguided speculation.

I was 29, living in suburban West Ealing with a wife and, by then, two children. The group were 21-year-olds to whom someone eight years their senior would have seemed like Methuselah. The fundamental element in the relationship was that I didn't confuse myself with the group. Some publicists became infatuated with the reflected prestige of their charges. This did not interest me, so it is difficult to conjecture what licentious excesses might have followed had I strayed into that sphere. I perceived myself, perhaps delusionally, as an uncomplicated man with a stable personal life who loved popular music and could speak for and about the people he represented on behalf of the company. It was routine at this stage – and later, after the Sex Pistols had broken up, and Sid and his girlfriend Nancy Spungen were misbehaving in hotel rooms – for me to receive calls from national newspapers in the middle of the night requesting clarification or comment on the latest allegation about the group on which they were about to go press. My baby daughter Louise occasionally woke up during such conversations, and I would rock her back to sleep while confirming, denying or qualifying some real or imagined story.

It was around this time that I also began receiving telephone threats from a man announcing himself as Crazy Legs, who felt he had a duty as a "rocker" to rid the world of punks, especially if this might reflect heroically on him among his peers. Unable to locate the most famous punks in the world, he had decided to transfer his attention to me, and, as such people invariably do, he claimed to know where I lived.

"Rotten" and "Vicious" were indicative of the kind of car-toonish posturing that was fundamental to the punk era, whose adoption of emotive surnames probably began with Richard Hell, a punk pioneer, a little older than the others, but well into the subsequently adopted iconography of torn clothes, spiky hair and safety pins. The British entrepreneur Larry Parnes had once given such high-powered suffixes to his entire stable of singers – Billy Fury, Marty Wilde, Vince Eager, Dickie Pride, Duffy Power, Johnny Gentle – but Hell was probably the first one to change his own surname to something he thought made a statement about him. Virgin also signed a band called The Motors, whose first album was released a couple of months before the Sex Pistols'. The newspaper ad for it featured the actress Jayne Mansfield – who had died, decapitated, in a 1967 car accident – with the speech balloon "I lost my head over the Motors" emerging from her mouth. For some, this reinforced the perception that Virgin had completely surrendered to punk outrage. Sometime between conception and release, the Motors' guitarist, whom I had met as Peter Bramall, and their drummer, introduced to me as Richard Wernham, had metamorphosed into Bram Tchaikovsky and Ricky Slaughter respectively. We had several unattractively named bands as well, engineered to offend. We distributed four singles by the Dead Kennedys. My favourite was their final one for us, "Too Drunk to Fuck", supported by a reliably provocative promotional t-shirt that certainly struck up conversation in crowded bars.

While an album of Sex Pistols recordings was accumulating, another single was released – "Pretty Vacant", their most compelling song, for which they filmed an on-stage promo (with no audience) one morning at the Marquee, enabling them to appear on television without prompting the unrest with which they were now inescapably associated. McLaren had also visited Los Angeles during the summer, to oversee the evolving script of a film being written by the critic Roger Ebert and director Russ Meyer – their office a room at the Sunset Marquis hotel – who had collaborated successfully on the remarkable *Beyond the Valley of the Dolls* seven years earlier. Its title was *Who Killed Bambi?*, and accordingly it contained a scene in which an arrow is fired from a bow and kills a deer. Ebert had not heard of the Sex Pistols when Meyer called him about working together on the project, which was to be financed by 20th Century Fox and filmed in England. One day in October, McLaren – whose arrivals in our office had the impact of a sudden whirlwind – came in to inform us that there was a problem. Fox, he said, had withdrawn its financing because Princess Grace of Monaco (once 1950s screen goddess Grace Kelly), a Fox board member, had opposed bankrolling a film which featured the group that had famously insulted her close friends, the British royal family. Then Russ Meyer himself had resigned, after shooting only the deer-hunting scene. This was the remarkable speed at which life now operated in the group's world. A year later, after they had broken up as a functioning entity and the Sex Pistols were just a concept – mixing and matching the remaining members – there would be a completely different Sex Pistols film called *The Great Rock'n'Roll Swindle*, which Virgin helped to finance. (Ebert later posted the entire *Who Killed Bambi?* script on his blog in 2010. It's startling, one of its highlights a scene in which guitarist Steve Jones receives oral sex from a hooker while consuming a hamburger.)

For the moment, though, there were more bans and boycotts to deal with, and, we learnt, a vigilante anti-Pistols group in Scotland. There was another single, "Holidays in the Sun" – whose second-line reference to the concentration camp Belsen was considered unacceptably confronting for broadcast on Capital Radio – and finally an album called *Never Mind the Bollocks, Here's the Sex Pistols*, whose title alone was considered too offensive to be seen in WH Smith, Boots and Woolworths, and also included the song "God Save the Queen", which these stores had already banned months earlier. A shop manager in Nottingham who defied the order was charged under the 1889 Indecent Advertisement Act. Two others in London were accused of contravening the indecent advertisements section of the 1824 Vagrancy Act. A fourth did not have any century-old act invoked, but was visited by police and instructed to cover up the word "Bollocks" in his window display. We took on John Mortimer QC, well acquainted with such cases since the 1970 *Oz* trial, to defend the store managers. Meanwhile, rumours abounded of secret Sex Pistols gigs – and were sometimes true.

Incapable of avoiding controversy by this stage – instead, having become a magnet for it – Virgin also took on Derek and Clive, the foul-mouthed alter egos of Peter Cook and Dudley Moore. They had already made one outrageous album that had become a byword for the unspeakable. The *Daily Mirror* acquired an early copy of our follow-up, *Derek and Clive Come Again,* and ran a piece headlined DISC-GUSTING outlining the various subjects discussed on the record – sodomy, incest, homosexuality, masturbation, cancer, cannibalism and murder – and the several dead celebrities (Joan Crawford, Bertrand Russell, Pablo Picasso) on whom Derek and Clive speculated uninhibitedly. "One particular four-letter word", the *Mirror* declared, appalled, "is used 174 times". This forensic analysis was reinforced by their discovery that quality control staff at the pressing plant refused to continue checking sample records. Peter's response to the media was – "If you buy a record which carries a warning that it contains filthy language then you know roughly what you are buying". Mine was that it contained no redeeming social value whatsoever, and that I didn't anticipate much radio play.

A further obstacle arose when CBS – which had agreed to distribute the album – then decided not to. Anxious about being prosecuted for obscenity, they gave us a week's notice, so we hastily needed to improvise an alternative. Mortimer was back on board with an opinion – that the material was "not obscene in that it is too farcical, absurd and funny to have the slightest tendency to deprave and corrupt anyone". However, we did stop mailing the album to anyone, in case sending it by post might open the gate to police action. I received various letters of complaint from members of the public saying that between this and punk rock, we were scum-sucking bottom-feeders – although one of them did add winningly "I'm sure that personally you are a very nice man."

When the discs of *Come Again* finally materialised, Peter and Dudley were away writing together in a mysteriously riot-torn Bermuda, so I organised a bawdy, surreal shambles of a press conference for London media via a malfunctioning transatlantic link and a small speaker on a low-slung coffee table, with the journos and me and Peter's wife Judy Huxtable gathered in the old Branson house around the corner from the office. Peter shifted seamlessly into his "Clive" gear, but couldn't quite conceal his surprise to discover his spouse on the line along with a roomful of rowdy hacks, by then sounding as if they were all sharing a jacuzzi in a resort spa with very poor acoustics. Afterwards, professional etiquette prompted me to resist mentioning to Judy the tremendous impact she'd had on a 20 year-old me when I saw her in a film called *The Touchables*. I had the feeling she might have heard this before, from other men who once used be 20. There was one more record to come from Derek and Clive – *Ad Nauseam*, its cover photo a transparent sick bag with contents. After that, there was really nowhere left for us to go.

As the year accelerated to a close, it felt as if someone had begun it by firing a starting pistol, and that after hearing the shot I had never looked up, even though at one point during it, I found two weeks of simple, magical stillness in Menorca with my family, every day exactly and perfectly the same. The Pistols were about to tour America for the first time – a handful of dates, most of them in the southern states, with their US record company Warner Bros looking after the arrangements. On December 30, the group's visa applications were declined by the American Embassy in London. By mid-afternoon December 31 US time, after Warner lawyers had spent the morning pleading with American immigration officials at the State Department in Washington, they had what they needed.

I thought there could be a few surprises to follow during the tour – and, of course, there were. British bands often had adjustment difficulties, both personal and cultural, to touring life in the US, oscillating between bedazzlement and hostility, with stop-offs at all points between. The shows (in Atlanta, Memphis, San Antonio, Baton Rouge, Dallas and Tulsa) played out satisfactorily to audiences fuelled more by curiosity than enthusiasm. Some of the elite media reporters who had flown down at their own expense from New York and Los Angeles seemed struck by the group's crude performing style, unavoidable since only guitarist Steve Jones and drummer Paul Cook could actually play their instruments, while Sid Vicious improvised around whatever bass notes came to him. As his notoriety had grown, so too had his heroin dependency, and his relationship with the American audiences became increasingly abusive in both directions. As the bottles and cans began to fly onto the stage, the imminent implosion of the group was becoming uncontainable.

McLaren appeared quite happy to witness this, even to stir it. He declared to reporters that he encouraged a climate of unrest within the band and viewed Sid as a troublesome catalyst who kept the others on their toes. It was a cold dark January of short days and short fuses. They were being monitored by the FBI, McLaren claimed, and travelled in a luxury bus with eight bunks, which allegedly belonged to Evel Knievel, who was unable use it because he was in jail at the time.

It was shortly after the last show at Winterland in San Francisco – which ended with John famously taunting the audience ("Ever get the feeling you've been cheated?") – that we heard the news that the group had finally fallen apart, certainly in the form that existed. Steve and Paul were soon on a flight to Rio to record with the fabled fugitive of 1963's Great Train

Robbery, Ronnie Biggs, another outlaw. Sid had gone to New York, the epicentre of heroin; John to London.

The death of punk was officially announced in the *Daily Mail* on January 20, 1978. The next trend, they said, was going to be something called Power Pop.

CHAPTER EIGHT

Despite the announcement and subsequent speculation, it was difficult to be sure if the Sex Pistols had truly, completely and irreversibly broken up. In the capricious world of group dissolutions – considering the generally unbalanced condition of the individual members of a band at such a time – it was not unknown for them to declare finality then discover quite quickly that life without their colleagues was not as liberating, rewarding and ego-inflating as they had anticipated. In the absence of reliable confirmation from Malcolm McLaren, I improvised my response to media, sometimes saying that, since the group members were in different corners of the world, it was impossible to be absolutely certain that they had split; at other times, that it may be an apt moment for them to break up because, with their success, they were in danger of outliving their usefulness – which was to be a thorn in the side of the big heaving beast of authority.

McLaren said that John had been fired from the group for being divisive. John said he had simply refused to go to Brazil with Steve and Paul to record with Ronnie Biggs – whose Brazilian girlfriend Raimunda's pregnancy had enabled him to escape extradition from Rio to a UK jail – because he considered it a hackneyed publicity stunt. Sid said nothing because he was barely capable of speech, having ended up in a New York hospital following a mid-flight drug coma.

Richard Branson invited John to accompany him and various others to Jamaica to consider reggae acts for Virgin's specialist label Front Line, no doubt hoping that along the way the possibility of getting the Pistols back together again could become a reality. He had made a substantial investment in the group, and naturally hoped they would be triumphant long-distance runners who might rise from the ashes of the break-up to become successors to the Rolling Stones. When they returned from the trip, John instead formed a new group, Public Image Ltd, who had no interest in doing this, but who continued to record for Virgin.

Steve and Paul recorded two tracks with Biggs as vocalist in Rio, and completed them in London. One was to be titled either "No One is Innocent" or "Cosh the Driver", the latter calibrated to cause offence, since the eponymous driver never fully recovered from the brain damage caused by the iron bar the Great Train Robbers hit him with. (The second song, "Belsen Was a Gas", was consigned to the film *The Great Rock'n'Roll Swindle* and its sound-track.)

"No One Is Innocent", the title sensibly decided, was released as a single, with Sid Vicious's rendition of "My Way" on the other side. This great French song by Claude François, given a valedictory twist in the English lyrics by Paul Anka, became both a climax and an epilogue to punk, its crowning achievement and, as it turned out, a coda to Sid's own life. With French session players, a ferocious guitar overdub from Steve Jones and a propulsive string arrangement by Simon Jeffes, Sid performs it on the stage of the fabled Olympia in Paris, descending its illuminated staircase in a white tuxedo to carry out the ultimate act of deconstruction on a song. It's a work of anarchic genius. In the video (and eventually the film), he concludes the performance by gunning down most of his bejewelled toff audience, including the Pistols' French label head Eddie Barclay. Anka would no doubt have been surprised to hear the third line of his lyric ("My friend, I'll say it clear") replaced by "you cunt, I'm not a queer". Subsequent writing royalties, and yet another lease of life for the song, may have made the change more palatable for François.

Sid was increasingly troubled – and in trouble – that summer, getting into several public fights which often involved his American girlfriend and fellow heroin addict, Nancy Spungen, with whom it was invariably love or war. I heard about the problems because the calls from newspapers in the middle of the night had re-started, and my children, now a year older, were again woken by them. Then in October, by this stage living in New York, Sid was charged with murdering Nancy at the Chelsea Hotel. He was arrested and taken to Rikers Island prison, among the most violent correctional facilities anywhere, and therefore one in which a celebrity bad-boy was unlikely to last long. The story contained exactly the cocktail of drugs, death and degradation that the media found irresistible, so the reports followed the classic pattern. First, belittle and devalue your subject, then propose speculation to support the claim – that it was the attention of an exploitative record company, mercenary Machiavellis such as us, which turned the Sex Pistols into a problem, disregarding that it was the press itself which tirelessly chronicled the group's every move and gave rise to much of the mythology surrounding them. All we knew was that Sid needed bail posted urgently and that we had the means to provide it. So we paid. It was not one of our better-timed ideas. Following his release, he overdosed and died at a party organised by his mother and new girlfriend to celebrate his freedom, his own mother allegedly administering the fatal dose. He was 21.

Although completing and distributing *The Great Rock'n'Roll Swindle* took another year – when it opened, *Variety* proclaimed it "the *Citizen Kane* of rock'n'roll movies" – essentially it was all over for the Sex Pistols. In most respects, this had been the case since the break-up at the end of the US tour, but McLaren had developed the idea of turning the abandoned Russ Meyer/Fox film into a self-aggrandising mockumentary about pop culture exploitation, with himself as the central character. And un-questionably, this is what he was: inventive, playful, resilient, ruthless, with a feel for mischief so evolved that it was practically supernatural.

My abiding memory of him is this: late in the day we're having a conversation in my office overlooking the cobblestoned yard in which Virgin's offices are located, the view extending to Portobello Road 50 metres away. A taxi he has ordered draws up at the end of the yard. Anxious that it might drive away without him, he tries to accelerate his pace towards it. A feature of the red tartan "bondage" trousers he's wearing is that they have a little strap between the legs, which impede running. So he ends up waddling tentatively up the yard in the direction of the waiting taxi, a swaggering punk entrepreneur suddenly made comically vulnerable by the restrictions of his clothing. "I invented the Sex Pistols to sell trousers," he later boasted. "And I sold a *lot* of trousers".

When the film was finished, I phoned Biggs to ask if he would do some phone interviews to help promote it, his response was intriguing, as if he had time-travelled to the cash-in-a-suitcase Tin Pan Alley of 20 years earlier. As well as appearing in the movie, he had contributed the lead vocal to a successful single released under the group's name. He said that he would talk to the press if he was paid the money that Malcolm McLaren owed him. I replied that the Sex Pistols' affairs were now in the hands of a receiver, Russell Hawkes of Spicer and Pegler, and that whatever he was due would need to come from there. I added that I thought it unlikely that a receiver would be well disposed to sending money to a man wanted by the British police for nearly two decades. Why then, he asked, did I not bring the cash to Rio myself? He would ensure I'd enjoy myself while I was there. I explained why not. With a final flourish, he said there might something else he could have instead. "The record was in the top 5 of the Hit Parade, right?" I explained that it was no longer called the Hit Parade, but yes. "Well," he replied, "I always understood that if you reached the top 5, you got a house and a car."

By this stage I had working with me two press officers, Linda Gamble and Sally Cooper, whose considerable social skills were reinforced by efficiency and good judgement, enabling me to be out of the office for days, occasionally weeks at a time.

A record company publicist spends endless time with bands on tour, orchestrating interviews, providing sympathetic company, showing solidarity, monitoring progress, observing audiences, being simultaneously a spectator and an adviser, along the way oscillating between great excitement and acute tedium. There were other Virgin acts I admired, enjoyed travelling with and watched repeatedly in clubs, concert halls and, in one case, cathedrals – all of them original thinkers, absorbing performers and often entertaining company – but without question the most fun I ever had with a group over the years, and the most pleasure I got from watching them succeed, was with XTC.

They were from Swindon in Wiltshire, and before they began recording and touring, only one of them had ever been out of England before, on a school trip to France. That a group which came together with a solitary passport between them were soon performing with such unswerving commitment in so many locations around the world reflected their willingness to throw themselves into the deranged vortex of travel and touring required of a band at the time, and for those of us who joined

110

them, there was always hilarity in their slipstream, their humour tireless and unremitting. The more foreign and extreme the location, the more they would amp up their West Country accents to remind themselves of who they were as the experiences became increasingly surreal and overwhelming.

A profile of XTC in *NME* listed 11 winning characteristics of the perfect band – youth, experience, energy, wit, professionalism, sharpness, weirdness, accessibility, addictiveness, sociability, modesty – and identified XTC as the group that had them all. On their first European tour they supported – and struck up a friendship with – the great American band Talking Heads, who were performing most of the songs from their debut album *Talking Heads 77* and road-testing those that would become *More Songs About Buildings and Food*. They were enthralling to watch, which we did most nights, sitting spellbound at small bar tables near the stage as they worked their way through David Byrne's ingenious compositions. Recognising XTC as kindred musical spirits and revelling in their grounded lack of self-importance, Talking Heads later invited them to be the opening group at their first major US concert at the Beacon Theatre in New York on New Year's Eve 1978/79. To cover their travel costs and their modest lodgings at the Iroquois Hotel on 44th Street, XTC also played three nights at the squalidly venerable CBGB and one at the Star Club in Philadelphia, a city with what appeared to be a nativity scene and a disco of pulsing Christmas lights in every suburban garden we drove past. It was the first time in the US for all of us, which heightened the absurdity of the situations in which we constantly found ourselves.

There was practically nowhere in the world which was wired up for electricity that XTC didn't tour, and where their intoxicating mix of melodic flair, playful dexterity and unselfconscious energy didn't have an impact. Although the world was opening up, countries like Australia, Japan and Venezuela – which the group would soon visit – still seemed a long way away.

Flying to Australia in the late 1970s, there were three stopovers – Bahrain, Kuala Lumpur, Singapore – and an airport press conference on landing in Sydney was a mandatory indication of status, despite the grinding banality of the questions and the incoherent fatigue of the replies. Their first show was at the Marconi Club in the western suburb of Fairfield, where a full-scale gold-rush brawl broke out within five minutes of our arrival. This should not have come as a surprise after the doorman had weighed the cake I had brought in to celebrate drummer Terry Chambers' birthday to establish that there were no concealed weapons baked into it. The second night was at a converted cinema in Manly called Flicks. After the show, we were invited to the nearby penthouse apartment of its promoter, who appeared to have employed Liberace's interior designer. It was decorated almost entirely in white – white walls, white shag pile, white grand piano, several platinum blonde Lana Turner lookalikes dressed in white. We sat on the white sofa under the only thing in the apartment that wasn't white – a panoramically long mounted crocodile skin under which the promoter has joined us, raising a lazy eyebrow towards the lifeless reptile above and declaring "I caught it. I fucked it. I skinned it." This was our introduction to our host for the evening – Larry Danielson, a jaw-dropping caricature of a certain kind of rough-as-guts folkloric Australian who might've inspired the creation of Les Patterson had Barry Humphries not already invented him. As Larry knocked back the whisky, he became increasingly withering towards his other guests and more insistent that we stay for longer, which we did until the first sunlight hit the coastal water.

Wondering when his name would show up again, and in what context, I enquired about him occasionally when I was back in London. Eighteen months after our encounter, I heard. A couple of extortionists were planting bombs in various branches of Woolworths in Sydney, and threatening others if they weren't given $1m, half in unmarked notes, half in gold bullion and diamonds. They were caught. One of them was Larry.

After six years of secluded living and immobilising panic attacks, Mike Oldfield transcended. He had finished recording an epic double album called *Incantations* and arrived in my office one day – clean-shaved, short-haired and smartly dressed, exactly as he appeared on the Menorcan beach of the album cover photo – to declare that, contrary to his custom of media avoidance, he wanted to do press interviews. Lots of them – as many as we considered useful, which he suggested be conducted in the back of a chauffeured Bentley driving around London. As for pictures, interesting ideas were always welcome. When the photographer Chalkie Davies proposed a series of naked studies in his studio – one of the well-known Greek sculpture of the discus thrower, another of Rodin's *The Thinker* – Mike was immediately intrigued and, once convinced, removed his clothes without further discussion, responding well to direction as these remarkable pictures were taken.

The catalyst for this striking shift of perspective had been his recent completion of a self-transformation course called Exegesis, which in part involved recreating the (it turned out) painful circumstances of his own birth, in doing so achieving a catharsis which eliminated the fear of the world – and of himself – that once inhibited him so acutely. He had emerged from this with the wind in his sails, although not in an evangelical or doctrinaire way: he was simply a bold, funny, playfully extroverted version of himself, unperturbed by anxiety or by appearing foolish, and therefore able to do anything he wanted. He had also married Exegesis founder Robert D'Aubigny's sister but was already in the process of divorcing her, and would soon set up house with Sally Cooper, leaving me a press officer short.

He wanted to tour as well. Live appearances – out of the question at the time of *The Orchestral Tubular Bells*, when other guitarists stood in for him – were back on the agenda. And not just any old tour, but one involving around 75 musicians, choir and crew, to play sports stadiums in Barcelona and Madrid, then concerts in Paris, Dusseldorf and Berlin, before proceeding through Belgium, the Netherlands and Denmark, returning to Germany for more shows, and climaxing with a triumphant return to England, where – as was the case everywhere he went – very few people had actually seen him play. The choir was a dozen of David Bedford's singing pupils from Queens College. Reinforced by his friendship with Mike and forensic familiarity with his music, this made him the ideal conductor for the tour. Sally Arnold had been a recent Rolling Stones tour manager, so was accustomed to orchestrating an army, which this was. She was also a trained nurse and nanny, an unexpected bonus when childish behaviour can be anticipated in a touring party.

I acted as interpreter at Spanish press conferences, and managed visiting journalists. My return to Spain following a decade of absence came soon after its first democratic election since the civil war, and the country was in a heightened state of vitality, confidence and release.

Although there were parts of the lengthy *Incantations* which prompted me to take the occasional recreational walk around the perimeter of the crowd during the first half of the concert, it was often exhilarating to witness the pleasure and assurance with which Mike presented his music to such large crowds following all the years of stage fright. These were wonderful performances, and the remarkable media coverage they generated was compounded by surprisingly candid turns taken in his interviews. When he told Allan Jones of *Melody Maker* – a man whose hilarious unblinking accounts of extreme behaviour in music circles were the stuff of legend – that the end of Side 1 of his album *Ommadawn* was the sound of him exploding from his mother's vagina, Jones clearly needed a cold compress and a lie-down.

Other than once having my back walked on by a beautiful Japanese interpreter in the middle of the transit lounge at Anchorage airport, one of the ancillary pleasures of the many hours of travel to which I was becoming accustomed was the remarkable amount of reading I could complete on each journey if I disregarded food, sleep and in-flight movies. I would decide on a writer – first F. Scott Fitzgerald, then Raymond Chandler – and work my way through everything they had written and, for the most part, had been written about them. No short story or essay escaped me, and no accessible account of their lives went unread. It was the same complete saturation that I had applied to popular music, the legacy of a solitary childhood.

When I had finished reading Chandler – or at least his seven novels – I thought there might be a book in a detailed analysis of the film adaptations of all but one of these, together with chapters on his fabled original screenplay (*The Blue Dahlia*) and his collaborations with Billy Wilder (on James M. Cain's *Double Indemnity*) and Alfred Hitchcock (on Patricia Highsmith's *Strangers on a Train*). I had also heard about a romantic drama (*And Now Tomorrow*) and a supernatural thriller (*The Unseen*) he had written during his brief period as a professional screenwriter.

Prompted by Chandler's descriptive and geographical precision – his characters invariably drove along particular roads towards specific destinations – I had also become fascinated with Los Angeles as a city, intensified by my first visit there accompanying a journalist and photographer from *NME* on a story about the group Devo, who were signed to Virgin outside the US. I was reading Rayner Banham's extraordinary *Los Angeles* (the finest book ever written about the history, architecture and topography of a city) as we flew over the desert on the final leg of the flight from London, and when we landed in the late afternoon, I realised there was only one person there that I knew. It was Nancy Dowd, whose brilliantly foul-mouthed script of *Slap Shot* I had admired and who had recently won an Oscar for *Coming Home*. Nancy had been in London at the height of punk about 20 months earlier, researching a world she was writing about for record producer Lou Adler's second (and final) film as a director – which was to feature a punk band. This ended up being her pseudonymous screenplay (credited to "Rob Morton") of the barely released *Ladies and Gentlemen, the Fabulous Stains* with, as the band, Steve Jones and Paul Cook of the Sex Pistols, Paul Simonon of the Clash, and – it seems unbelievable now – Ray Winstone as the lead singer.

So, newly arrived and still a day away from renting a Cadillac Fleetwood convertible the length of a city block, I took a taxi to Nancy's house. The driver followed numerous winding roads up into the hills, and soon we were in prototype *noir* territory, but I didn't realise quite how close to the Hollywood sign we were until I found myself in the warm night air swimming in a pool which appeared to be directly beneath it. So there I was. On my first night in Los Angeles, I held the Oscar that was on Nancy's mantelpiece, shot the jet-lagged breeze with her guest Viva –

whom I recognised from Andy Warhol films – and drank wine under the Hollywood sign in a city already in my bloodstream. Hallucinatory.

I wanted more of this. And, a few months later, I got it.

CHAPTER NINE

The Montecito Hotel did not engender confidence. It was a Sunday night and the weekend foot traffic appeared to have left indelible traces on the lobby carpet, which had seen better days. So had the receptionist, a tape over one lens of his spectacles and a practiced vacant manner, as if giving you his full attention might be misconstrued as a weakness. Hovering silently in the background, a resentful-looking middle-aged man in a white tie who looked as if he might one day wake up with an ice pick in his neck.

The entire hotel interior was textbook Raymond Chandler – crumbling California stucco, overflowing ashtrays, faded and fatigued furniture – a feeling of history silently evaporating in the memory, despite the declaration in its brochure, clearly printed some years earlier, of being the "hotel of the stars". It also claimed to be the highest building in Hollywood in elevation. Accordingly, there was an incandescent view from my 12th floor corner suite, its windows facing in every direction, revealing an endless unrolling display of lights below, with a sprinkle of architectural follies tucked into the hills above Franklin Avenue behind. There was no question about where you were.

A wander down to an unexpectedly quiet Hollywood Boulevard – its crown jewel, the restaurant Musso & Frank, closed on Sundays – revealed an immediate galaxy of strangeness in the street life. A tall black man miming to a nursery rhyme and so affecting a small child's voice and posture, with a white-suited Superfly figure in attendance. A pizza shop named Two Guys from Italy, populated entirely by chattering Hispanics. An animal hospital with a neon sign outside, as if it were a motel or a strip club.

I was there thanks to my school friend – and, more recently, my Edinburgh Festival Fringe theatre impresario – Don Boyd, with whom I had recently become reacquainted. In the intervening years he had become a successful film producer and had recently moved to Los Angeles, with a rented house above Sunset Plaza and an office at what was then Goldwyn Studios, where he was setting up a very expensive American comedy, *Honky Tonk Freeway*, with the British director John Schlesinger. He had agreed to sponsor a research trip, with an assistant, for my proposed book about Raymond Chandler's life in film – either as the provider of source material or as a screenwriter between 1943 and 1950 – an idea I had set in motion after my first trip to California a few months earlier.

While aware that one required a car there, my first two taxi rides demonstrated what I might be missing in daily human interaction. One driver, an old native Angeleno, revealed himself to be an improbable admirer of the British comedian Benny Hill ("that guy is *so* funny"); the other told me he had been served his breakfast in a diner that morning by a waitress who claimed to have fellated James Mason at the Beverly Wilshire hotel in 1953.

The assistant and I were duly installed in the publicist Dennis Davidson's offices in Beverly Hills and set about contacting survivors of Chandler-related films who might contribute their memories and insights to interviews with me. The saturation filmgoing of my solitary childhood had served me well, because I required little background information on any of them. I felt I knew who these people were. The first revelation was the proximity of one of them. The office directly below mine was occupied by the celebrated Swifty Lazar who, in addition to being Lauren Bacall's agent (and therefore someone whose cooperation I was seeking), was also a character in what may be my favourite Hollywood story – one about the calibration of meals – that most simply illustrates the unspoken lines of perceived social status which cannot be crossed without reprimand.

The characters in it are Joseph Heller, the renowned author of *Catch 22*, his agent Lazar, and the noted television producer David Wolper. At the peak of his success, fielding offers for highly-paid movie scripts, Heller flew into LAX one day and called Lazar from an airport payphone to arrange a meeting during his few days there. Lazar was very excited by this and proposed that they have dinner that evening. Heller explained that he already had a dinner arranged. Lazar asked who with. Heller said David Wolper. Lazar went silent for a second, then simply couldn't restrain himself: "David Wolper", he sneered. "But David Wolper's a LUNCH!"

I was plainly not Joseph Heller, so when I asked Lazar if he would give me Lauren Bacall's phone number or otherwise enable me to speak to her, the surviving star of *The Big Sleep*, he abruptly refused. Since his clients past and present also included Clifford Odets, Cole Porter, Irwin Shaw, Vladimir Nabokov and Tennessee Williams, it did occur to me that helping an unknown writer gain access to his prestigious charges was unlikely to be a high priority for him. So I called someone else. Mysteriously, the someone else would pass on Bacall's number to me only on the understanding that I tell her that it was given to me by Billy Wilder, as Bacall would be bound to ask. So I honoured the agreement. Only in Hollywood, as I was learning to say, where lotus seekers and lotus eaters coalesced and mutated, where officious public notices abounded (do this, don't do that) and where a ubiquitous advertisement alerted the public to the unavoidable prospect of earthquakes, instructing us all to be "Quake-Aware".

When I discovered that four directors and five writers on my list were already dead, the pursuit of those still alive, particularly the septuagenarians, became more urgent, and their recollections correspondingly more vital before they faded or disappeared entirely. In the end, it all balanced out. For every Billy Wilder who no longer wanted to talk about the making of *Double Indemnity*, there was a Fred MacMurray who did. James Garner claimed to have no relevant recollections of the film *Marlowe* (based on Chandler's *The Little Sister*), but the candid and discursive Stirling Silliphant (screenwriter) and Paul Bogart (director) did. Lewis Allen (director of the Chandler-scripted *The Unseen*) and John Houseman (producer of this and Chandler's subsequent original screenplay *The Blue Dahlia*) were both eloquent and practised interviewees – and clearly disliked each other.

I tracked down Edward Dmytryk (director of *Murder My Sweet*, based on Chandler's *Farewell My Lovely*) to Austin Texas, where he was lecturing at the university, and spoke to him at length. I talked to the film's screenwriter John Paxton in a cafe around the corner from my office. I met George Montgomery (who played Chandler's detective Philip Marlowe in *The Brasher Doubloon*, the film adaptation of his novel *The High Window*) and Philip Carey (Marlowe in the television series), separately, in a Beverly Hills bar. When they ran out of stories about the subject in hand, I knew their work well enough to navigate the conversation somewhere else. Montgomery, whom I had seen in numerous westerns, was an interesting case: still strikingly handsome in his 60s, dressed all in denim with turquoise jewellery, and flirting with the waitresses. With him, I commented on Lynn Bari, who appeared in *The Falcon*

Takes Over, the first film adaptation of *Farewell My Lovely*. He had evidently lost contact with her – his co-star in *China Girl* 37 years earlier – and when I mentioned that she had been unable to meet me because of illness, a fleeting shadow clouded his gaze, somehow making him look older and more conscious of loss.

Then there was a lunch at a convivial show business restaurant called Orlando Orsini with Barry Sullivan, who appeared in *And Now Tomorrow*, a screenplay adaptation Chandler wrote while under contract to Paramount. Looking across the table at him, by then grey-bearded and playfully patriarchal, I remembered queuing to see him in Samuel Fuller's *Forty Guns* – outside a cinema in Bellshill, near my aunt's home south of Glasgow – when I was 10, wondering if its A (for adult) certificate and a management statement about unaccompanied minors might prevent me from getting in. (It didn't.) When his recollections of *And Now Tomorrow* ran out, we reminisced about *Forty Guns*, and about another of my heroes, Jimmy Webb, the great songwriter then married to one of Sullivan's daughters, Patsy.

And there was breakfast with a charming Audrey Totter, who was very much in evidence as the leading lady of *Lady in the Lake*. The camera is Philip Marlowe's point-of-view throughout and, except when taking beatings from villains, she is constantly in his sights. She had mostly retired from acting by this stage, and had been married for many years to a dentist called Leo Fred, so at the coffee shop where we met she was known simply as Mrs Fred.

The entire process took on an increasingly surreal resemblance to detective work, with me as the insistent private eye and the prospective interviewees as the reluctant suspects. I very much wanted to talk to Robert Mitchum, who played Philip Marlowe twice – in the 1970s remakes of *Farewell My Lovely* and *The Big Sleep*. I had heard he was a garrulous sort, especially when he got stuck into the pear brandy. Some of his interviews, punctuated with unexpected surrealist comic touches, were very funny, although I had also heard he could be considerably less amusing if he turned. I wrote to him, asking if I might drive up to see him in Santa Barbara, despite his declared dislike of writers visiting his home. "If, as is rumoured", I added, "your greeting to strangers consists of mortar shells at chest height, we could meet in a nearby bar or park". I thought it was quite an entertaining and persuasive plea, but evidently he did not, as there was no reply.

Czenzi Ormonde – co-credited with Chandler for the screenplay (adapted from Patricia Highsmith's novel) of Alfred Hitchcock's *Strangers on a Train* – sent me a very long letter from the cattle ranch (letterhead The Ormonde Ranch) to which I had tracked her down in the middle of Idaho, her recollections surprisingly exact. She never met Chandler, she said, and began working on the script on the same day that Hitchcock held Chandler's draft over a waste bin and, with a flourish, dropped it in. Before becoming a writer herself, she had been an assistant to Ben Hecht – one of Hollywood's greatest and most prolific screenwriters – who had in recent years written *Spellbound* and *Notorious* for Hitchcock, and would therefore have provided a safety net if things had not worked out. They did, although Hecht is rumoured to have done some uncredited work on the film.

Towards the end of my stay in California, I finally located Nina van Pallandt – a wistful and indelible presence in Robert Altman's adaptation of Chandler's penultimate novel *The Long Goodbye*. Altman wanted his film to have a surreal, dreamy, pastel quality – suggesting Marlowe's perception of the city – in contrast to the squalid superficiality and opportunism of the 1970s Los Angeles which had eclipsed it. Van Pallandt, a Danish baroness new to films – although not to show business – had received considerable and unwelcome media attention from her perceived connection to the infamous literary hoax of Clifford Irving's bogus Howard Hughes biography shortly before Altman began casting. When he saw her interviewed by Johnny Carson one night, he felt sure he had found the perfect lead actress for his film. She was also the finest interviewee of all for my book – candid, clear-headed, communicative and kind.

As I was about to vacate my office in Beverly Hills, two interesting things occurred, the type that invariably happen while you're packing bags and leaving somewhere. One was that Alfred Hitchcock finally called me back, although in the end he didn't have much to say that I hadn't heard already. Still, there was that unmistakable *voice*, the most distinctive and best-known of any film director, one that no mimic has ever quite duplicated. The other was that I came to a realisation quite as unanticipated as the first-day discovery that Swifty Lazar's office was just under mine. Each weekday morning before noon, a young woman called Barbara, from her desk in the office next to mine, would have a cheerful and familiar phone conversation with the man she evidently lived with, whose voice was never on speaker and so was not audible. They would have talked about other things at other times during the day as well, but the usual objective of this particular exchange was to discuss dinner plans for the evening – in or out, food shopping or restaurant reservation, guests or not, and what time. Suggestions were made, modified, discussed, accepted.

In a fleeting farewell conversation with one of her work colleagues, I finally discovered the identity of the man who had been at the other end of the phone, inaudible to all but Barbara. He had one of the most recognised, impersonated and loved voices of the 20th century. It was Cary Grant.

CHAPTER TEN

I returned to Los Angeles a few months later to finish researching and start writing, this time on my own, staying in a small dark room at the Tropicana motel on Santa Monica Boulevard, the mandatory lodgings of rock groups touring on a restricted accommodation budget. There was a lively atmosphere around the small swimming pool, gleefully populated by people who didn't have one at home, and the ground floor included Duke's coffee shop, whose atmosphere, large portion sizes and food quality were as legendary as the motel they served. When Yoli and the children arrived to join me a few weeks later, I was moved at no extra charge to a bungalow once rented by Tom Waits on the adjacent side road.

I still travelled a good deal, often accompanying XTC and bringing with me a journalist able to write a long, entertaining account of their experience that was likely to result in a substantial cover feature on the group, as we continued trying to build on their success. This was sometimes Allan Jones of *Melody Maker*, whose sense of comic detail was unerring, and whose reports people who followed music weeklies actually read. Once we travelled in a van across America from Houston – where the group performed in an ocean of big hair, cowboy boots and Stetsons one evening – across all of Texas, New Mexico and Arizona to San Diego, California, to play to fifty people in a scout hut three nights later. Then there was a night supporting The Cars at Madison Square Garden, and the premiere of the film *Times Square*, sitting for two hours directly behind Lou Reed, whose enduring status as a New York landmark made it rather like being stranded under the Statue of Liberty; and finally there was the all-eclipsing Venezuelan craziness of Caracas, where XTC arrived from Miami half an hour before Prince Charles's royal flight landed at the airport to a blizzard of commotion. The group performed in a giant astrodome in a valley outside the city to an audience lighting bonfires with newspapers and police charging at them with bayonets. Stopped at traffic lights on the way back to the hotel, I looked across at the driver of the neighbouring car. He was stroking his stubble with the barrel of a handgun.

It was a remarkable time in live performance. When you entered a venue, you really had no idea what might happen, although you thought you did. Some months after Richard Pryor set himself on fire while freebasing cocaine and disappeared from the stand-up world, I was at the Comedy Store in Los Angeles when he showed up unannounced to reacquaint himself with playing to a crowd, which an incredulous audience treated as if witnessing a messianic resurrection. And I still went to see new bands, particularly those travelling in the slipstream of punk, with names guaranteed to offend. Over a couple of nights at RT Firefly in New York, I witnessed The Brattles, The Sic Fucks and The Reluctant Virgins – and made a note to check out The Bleeding Arseholes, The Slug Fuckers and I Spit On Your Gravy when I was next in Australia.

The Brattles were, as their name suggests, children. Even in such libertarian times, it was unusual to see people so young on stage hours after many of their contemporaries were asleep, attended by mothers and fathers in tight leather trousers and spiky hair acting as their roadies. A tragicomic highlight came when the bass guitarist, posturing enthusiastically with the neck of his instrument, thrust it into the mouth of the pallid and fragile looking lead singer, also in leather trousers, who began to cry and was rapidly comforted by his parents, who rushed on to the stage.

Despite such lively interludes, gradually but perceptibly the balance of my working life began to change. The round-the-clock devotion to being the answering machine for the Sex Pistols, dealing with every cough and splutter of the media, was receding, my representation of Virgin's groups still attentive but less micromanaged. The company was expanding in ways that enabled me to apply myself to other elements within it, re-igniting my curiosity in books and films. The Sex Pistols movie *The Great Rock'n'Roll Swindle* – which we had rescued from potential oblivion, invested in and set up distribution for – was finally completed and premiered at the London Pavilion, where both the Beatles films, *A Hard Day's Night* and *Help!*, had opened and played at for many weeks. Although Virgin had no experience in distribution, we believed that what would most determine the film's success was an understanding of the group's audience, which we had.

Its producer Jeremy Thomas and I talked about the possibility of filming Raymond Chandler's *Playback* – of whose unpublished screenplay I had obtained a copy, the only script he wrote based on his own work – but were mysteriously informed that the film rights, dormant for decades, were not available. I initiated and began preparing my first edition of *The Film Yearbook* for Virgin Books and became editor of *The Rock Yearbook* after the editor of the first one resigned. I wrote all the capsule reviews for *The Film Yearbook* myself. For longer pieces I made a list of movie critics I admired – some from my days as a young reader of *Films and Filming* (Raymond Durgnat, Mike Sarne), others more recent US encounters (Andrew Sarris, Dave Marsh) – and asked them to contribute. Apart from Pauline Kael – who declined on the grounds that the *New Yorker* already gave her however much space she wanted to write about whatever she wished – they all agreed.

Virgin as a whole was going through a difficult time in its evolution, mutating into other forms, diminishing the gung-ho adrenalin which had once invigorated the workload. Lengthy memos about new centralised financial control structures and management committees began appearing on my desk, together with timetables of proposed meetings between various combinations of individuals, procedures that are normal in most companies, but which consume energy and cause distraction. Newspaper articles appeared speculating about the company's fluctuating fortunes and perceived internal unrest, triggered by a number of redundancies and dismissals. These reports were wearying and demoralising to respond to constantly – which I felt a reflexive obligation to do.

During this time, Paula Yates was one of the people who most extended and brightened the landscape. I knew her a little as the girlfriend of Boomtown Rats singer Bob Geldof, whom I knew even less, and was struck by her coquettishness, chutzpah and unpredictability, a singular figure to collide with occasionally at concerts. She was ferociously intelligent, hilariously indiscreet, shamelessly manipulative and, I later discovered, the most entertaining of lunch companions.

She had famously done a photo spread for *Penthouse* magazine at the hallowed Reform Club, which was soon to open its doors to women for the first time, and where she sat naked on Oliver Cromwell's head, but by the time I met her properly she was taking the pictures herself, putting together a characteristically high-concept book of Polaroids called *Rock Stars in Their Underpants* for Virgin Books. She knew numerous rock stars already, and it did not take her long to persuade the ones she didn't know to pose for her book. She started with brothers Ron and Russell Mael from Sparks, who were recording for Virgin with Giorgio Moroder in Munich at the time, and took it from there. Elton John was in it. So were Rod Stewart, Paul McCartney, Chrissie Hynde, Debbie Harry and others. These candid, often unflattering photos were of their Polaroid moment, a world away from the retouching and photoshopping that would soon become routine.

She also had a weekly column in *Record Mirror*, one which usually focused on improbable encounters with pop music celebrities. Familiar with her sense of humour and low boredom threshold, I sometimes suggested ideas. One day we took a ride in a small plane piloted by Mike Oldfield, taking off and landing in an airfield near his house in Buckinghamshire, the kind of airfield where you had to be recommended by existing long-term members and ratified by a committee. Preceded by dozens of safety checks involving innumerable knobs and levers, we went up twice in different directions, the second landing a bumpy one in an escalating crosswind. Since his transformative self-realisation course a couple of years earlier, Mike had continued to work on confronting fears – flying had been one of them – and building self-confidence, so his new hobby was an extension of that.

On another occasion, I escorted Paula to Richard Branson's houseboat to have lunch with the noted French composer and performer Serge Gainsbourg and his girlfriend Bambu. Compared with Richard's previous lunch guest, Uri Geller, – who flamboyantly began bending the cutlery moments after we'd finished eating – Gainsbourg was a striking still-life silent guest. With a small, resilient UK fan base and residual notoriety from his recording with Jane Birkin, "Je T'Aime, Moi Non Plus" a decade earlier, he had written a novel – a short one and, as it turned out, an only one – which was about to be published by Virgin Books. It was titled *Evguénie Sokolov*, whose main character and narrator is a *Pétomane*-like character, an artist and compulsive farter who invariably blames his inseparable dog for his own persistent breaking of wind. "With fermentation and putrefaction in the caeco-colonic-rectal area being the major source of intestinal gases", he wrote, "I realised the prime importance of my diet". Gainsbourg's diet, on this occasion confined to wine and cigarettes, did not appear to have much importance at all. Nor was he interested in discussing his book. He said very few words, none of them sober. There wasn't much for Paula to report on, but she enjoyed the strangeness of the encounter and wrote about it anyway.

In a bid to expand and diversify, and despite the restraints on spending, Richard acquired a couple of clubs – The Venue in Victoria and The Roof Gardens in Kensington – but also, more significantly, had begun exploring seriously the prospect of a listings-based London magazine. He had intermittently entertained this notion over the years, but had not pursued it, perhaps subconsciously intimidated by the enduring dominance of *Time Out* across the previous decade. Now, however, its founder, editor and publisher Tony Elliott – once my employer – had hit a seemingly impenetrable wall. An industrial dispute over pay had closed down publication, and many of its staff were starting their own rival magazine, *City Limits*, whose first issue was already in advanced planning. Richard asked me if I would co-edit *Event*, as he had decided to name it, with Pearce Marchbank, whom I'd known when I was at *Time Out* a decade earlier, and whose design work I'd continued to admire in the interim. From the start, Fleet

Street newspapers were suspicious of *Event* and of what we aspired to do. I saw us as a London counterpart of *New York* magazine, equal parts reliable listings and high-quality writing, with one week perhaps a high-profile star on the cover and a news exclusive the next. Although I had edited the music section at *Time Out*, the *Guardian*'s correspondent was sceptical of my ability to make the magazine hum editorially. "But that is the Branson style," he ruminated. "He likes taking switchboard operators and making them marketing managers."

So I wrote a few farewell notes to my clients. These now included Phil Collins, whose astonishing first solo single "In the Air Tonight" and corresponding album *Face Value* had become enormous successes that marked a significant (and enduring) turning of the tide for Virgin Records; and Scott Walker, whom we had signed a year earlier but had yet to record. I was beginning to wonder if he would ever do so when he agreed to meet Brian Eno for a drink at the Kensington Hilton, in whose bar Scott and I occasionally got together to talk about films, jazz and comedy. It was a relationship uncomplicated by expediency, fuelled by mutual curiosity and a sense of the absurd. Eno had been interested in working with him ever since hearing Scott's compositions for the final Walker Brothers record *Nite Flights*, so I introduced them and left. They would eventually work together on an album, begun then aborted, three years later.

Then I dived straight into the dense labyrinth of creating and editing a new magazine in a short time. The hours were long, the office climate one of debilitating overdrive. When I finally came up for air on the eve of publication, we were not only about to compete with *Time Out* (which, in the meantime, had re-staffed and rebuilt) but *City Limits*, which in addition to the substantial cash support from the Greater London Council had, to some bewilderment, sent out brochures containing CVs and photos of its entire 46-person staff, prompting Paul Johnson to write in *The Spectator* – "One's first thought: why the hell do they need so many? Second thought: what a gruesome collection. Were all these snaps taken in a BR photomat?"

The day of reckoning came after just a few weeks of publication. Between the three magazines, the competition for readers was escalating to a point where, to attract attention and controversy, *Event* began to dig deeper and darker with news stories, and the editorial policy was straying into what I perceived to be sensationalist speculation. I was proved right when we had to make a full-page apology to a justly aggrieved party. The struggle for survival in a congested market had eclipsed all other considerations, and I increasingly felt the moral vacuum at our core. There was too much over-adrenalised power-mongering, too much arm wrestling over pits of scorpions, too much effort and energy expended on what wasn't appearing in the magazine and not enough on what was. Seven issues in, and in a state of chronic unrest, I resigned not only from the magazine but from the board of Virgin Records as well.

After such a comprehensive bridge-burning measure, one is never certain what feelings will follow. For me, the predominant one was – to paraphrase a laxative advertisement of the early 1960s – relief beyond belief. Although without a regular income for the first time in nearly a decade, I was oddly exhilarated by the absence of obligations, and I felt sure that the internecine warfare I had closely witnessed had revealed that I was the expendable element in the magazine which, beginning to leak from all parts, was to struggle through a few more months.

Over the period which followed, I anticipated completing my Raymond Chandler book, submitting it to publishers, its eventual publication and promotion – all of which would gradually materialise. Although the original publisher Proteus somehow managed to transpose two of its pages before it went to the printer, they did commission Daniel Kleinman – who went on to design the opening titles of the James Bond movies – to provide a wonderful cover illustration. It was a kind of enjoyment that could not have been replicated at Virgin, because it was something, I had accomplished myself. When later in the process, I went onstage to introduce some of the films during retrospective tie-ins at the Scala in London, Film House in Edinburgh, Tyneside Cinema in Newcastle or Phoenix Arts in Leicester, I was representing myself, and when perfectly presented extracts appeared in magazines such as *Time Out* and *The Face*, I had helped to put them there. Most enjoyable of all was an appearance on the Joe Franklin television chat show in New York, a venerated institution which ran continuously for 42 years. At the time I appeared on it, it had five million viewers.

But before all that, I decided that my initiative, my family's support of it, and our collective absence of fear about the immediate future should be rewarded by a holiday at the furthest away location to which we could still afford a flight. It turned out to be Key West in Florida, where we landed not long before midnight on New Year's Eve, the eve also of my daughter's sixth birthday. On a little jetty, with the moon on the water and the glow of festive fireworks, we celebrated – happy to be alive, where we were, and with each other.

We were certainly in some kind of heaven. It was the children's first seaside holiday since our Menorcan idyll of four years earlier, and they were in disbelieving rapture – channel surfing early morning American television from the moment they awoke, swimming in the hotel pool ten steps away from our room, riding the miniature train that transported tourists around the island, strolling along the little beach near the main pier, almost certainly the only pier in the world which encouraged people to gather on it each evening to applaud the sunset. One expects they still do, as they look southwest across the Gulf of Mexico towards Havana 100 miles away, aware that this sometimes forbidden fruit is closer than Miami.

On our second morning, the phone rang. Unbelievably, it was Tony Elliott, whose *Time Out* was now back on the rails and doing sufficiently well in the circulation war that he too had rewarded himself with a holiday. Having somehow heard that we had travelled to Key West and identified our lodgings, he was calling from a hotel across the road to suggest we meet up. There are few feelings as warmly satisfying as those when circum-stantially estranged old friends resume that friendship. He was accompanied by his girlfriend Janey, who – to complete the improbable jigsaw – had once worked at Virgin in various capacities, and whom I therefore knew well. We spent a delightful few days with them, irrigated by potent cocktails. All remained well with the world.

My flight had barely landed back in London when there was another phone call. This time it was Richard Branson, asking me to return to Virgin. He missed me, he said. He would invent a job for me. I could even make it up myself. Although his speech could be fractured and hesitant, he had a highly developed skill in making one feel wanted. This could sometimes take an oblique and mysterious turn. On a previous occasion when I had told him I intended to leave Virgin to take another job, he called my wife as I drove home from our meeting, pretending to be the managing director of the company from which I'd received the offer, and talked disconcerting nonsense.

My new role was to be the creative director of Virgin – all of it – responsible for broadening the sphere of our entertainment activities, and for exploring everything from original ideas to completed projects in books, records, films, television, theatre and whatever else came up. I was already committed to the *Rock* and *Film Yearbooks*, and had by then found an outside publisher for my book *Raymond Chandler in Hollywood*. What I was most interested in were things that didn't require much of an initial financial commitment from us but would enable us to learn and develop a presence in the relevant field. There were two ideas that intrigued me immediately. One was a version of *The Odyssey* to be performed on a boat and pontoon in the middle of the Thames. We passed on that one. The other was a short (25-minute) film based on Graham Greene's story *A Shocking Accident*, whose producer Christine Oestreicher and director James Scott had together already produced a short film (directed by Clare Peploe) called *Couples and Robbers*, which had been nominated for an Oscar that year.

When Christine introduced us to the principal financier of *A Shocking Accident*, Mamoun Hassan of the National Film Finance Corporation, his personable and persuasive manner bespoke the goodwill shown towards potential new sources of investment in the high-risk world of films. If it were a sufficiently painless first experience, we might understand the process better, want to do it again, and in doing so become producers ourselves. Although Virgin had earlier bailed out the Sex Pistols' film *The Great Rock'n'Roll Swindle*, this was different. I believed that the small amount required of us – just under £15,000 to enable completion of post-production – could prove quite significant by giving us an introduction to the movie business, and an increased practical understanding of it, at a very affordable cost.

After we had all agreed to go ahead, there was an unanticipated side benefit. I was in Los Angeles attending my first American Film Market, then driven predominantly by low-budget horror ("splatter matter") and movies that were proving difficult to sell to international distributors, such as Robert Towne's debut feature as a director, *Personal Best*, a film about two female runners who develop a lesbian relationship, pitched to me by its sales agent as "dykes on spikes". From my film-saturated childhood there remained a lingering curiosity about attending an Oscar ceremony, so when Christine called to say that, as the producer of *Couples and Robbers*, she was invited to the one about to take place, and that the director could no longer join her, I was at a tuxedo rental shop within moments.

In assembling the mandatory uniform – tux suit, white shirt, bow tie, cummerbund, shoes – I learnt that I was "standard Hollywood size", since everything fitted without adjustment. If you wear such an outfit any time after mid-morning on Oscar day everybody knows why, so they look at you for a second longer than usual, wondering where they may have already seen you, before quickly concluding that they never have, and that you're a nobody – but, of course, that you might know a somebody. On our ride to the presentations, then held at the Dorothy Chandler Pavilion downtown, our limo driver was John, a paragon of discretion with a highly trained radar for how much privacy was required and how much conversation. If you wanted to elope in the middle of the night, as people once did, he would drive you to Reno or Las Vegas and be freshly shaved before his morning assignment. Without question he would be on first name terms with all the hotel receptionists in Southern California.

One of the fundamental things to remember about the Academy Awards is that it's a live show – not so much an event which is covered by television as a television programme with very expensive extras playing themselves. When it stopped for an advertising break, the whole thing literally came to a halt, except for the stage sweepers and polishers, who meticulously maintained it for the cameras lest it lose its lustre over the marathon running time. The audience, far from being unsettled, had been on enough film sets to relish the familiarity of the short takes and long breaks, when they might wander out and check their appearance in the mirrored lobby, knowing that somebody would fill their seats in the meantime. I did it myself once, and found myself standing at a drinks cart next to Burt Bacharach and Angie Dickinson, by then divorced, but still the most perfect-looking show business couple of their era.

The host was Johnny Carson, who had been compering such shows for several years, reflected in his composed familiarity. In addition to the four veteran Hollywood scribes who "scripted" the show, which was difficult to discern beyond it having a running order, there were six "special material" writers – including, immodestly, Carson himself. His jokes weren't bad – a Pia Zadora one that could only have worked in that year of her notoriety ("Welcome to the Dorothy Chandler Pavilion. Next year it may be called the Pia Zadora Pavilion. We're just waiting for the cheque to come through") and running gags about the length of the ceremony ("In keeping with the trend towards nostalgia, try to cast your minds back to the beginning of the show"). His material, special and otherwise, varied in effectiveness but his timing was always impeccable.

Then there was my first slow-motion walk-past of Jack Nicholson, who appeared to be the dateless third wheel with Warren Beatty and Diane Keaton. Although superficially as uniformed and dandified as everybody else, he looked quite different, wearing shades – not the tastefully tinted aviator style popularised by 80s movies, but small round dark ones which allowed no access to the eyes they concealed. Also, his suit didn't fit properly – the trousers were too baggy, the jacket too tight. He resembled someone who had been in the middle of some other activity – gardening perhaps, or gambling – when the call had come through instructing him to get into a tuxedo, any tuxedo, and quickly get himself to the Dorothy Chandler Pavilion. Then there was the smile, one that managed to be open and shifty at the same time, participating in an event while observing its absurdities.

For a while though, even a bedazzled outsider would have had difficulty becoming excited during the acceptance speeches. There was the customary litany about creativity and collaboration. No one wanted to appear self-glorifying, so they recited lists – endless and apparently memorised ones of the many people who made their award possible – until the orchestra drowned them out. It all appeared to be lapsing into torpor until the Oscar for best foreign film was presented. This is statistically when the likeliest disregard for etiquette kicks in, particularly if the winning film is European. That night it was *Mephisto* by Hungarian director István Szabó, who called his lead actor Klaus Maria Brandauer out of the audience to the stage and engaged him in a long noisy bearhug.

A later much-parodied air-punching speech came from Colin Welland, writer of *Chariots of Fire*, and an inevitably mawkish one from Jane Fonda, whose father Henry won the best actor Oscar for *On Golden Pond* and was watching the broadcast at home, too frail to attend. Warren Beatty – who in his best director acceptance speech applauded capitalism for allowing a film like *Reds* to exist, and who was dignified in disappointment when it lost best picture to *Chariots of Fire* – did not resemble a man with a kidnap proof vault installed in his house, as I had heard earlier.

Entering the Governor's Ball at the Beverly Hilton, I crossed eyes with Gregory Peck who, as the crowd begin to shout his name, was looking for someone else in a tuxedo who might divert some of the attention he was getting. This clearly was not going to be me. Inside, I held another Oscar, this one belonging to *Raiders of the Lost Ark* editor Michael Kahn, with whom we shared a table. We stayed late, as we hadn't been invited to any of the after after-parties. Since *Couples and Robbers* had not won the award as best live action short, we toasted the prospect of returning with *A Shocking Accident* the following year. As we left, I noticed how quiet it was without the usual squadron of cars turning over outside, and I remembered Carson's great deadpan parting joke after the awards were over, when people were slowly filing out to their limos. This was the year when it appeared that everyone in the film business, whether successful or aspiring, owned a Mercedes. "There's a car blocking the entrance," Carson announced solemnly. "Does anybody here have a Mercedes?"

CHAPTER ELEVEN

Twelve days before I started a UK book tour, my marriage ended.

The underlying unrest had begun to reveal itself some time before, of course, and as the storm clouds unavoidably continued to gather, I travelled with Yoli and our daughter Louise, then seven, to Menorca – the setting of an idyllically contented holiday together only five years earlier – in what was intended as an attempt to repair the fractures I had caused in the relationship, but turned out to be a subconscious act of sabotage that ended up isolating us from both the world and each other. This time our lodgings were a bleak, draughty apartment block in Santo Tomas called the Vistamar, which appeared to offer neither *vista* nor *mar*, and to whose ground floor bar I would retreat after dinner each evening and sit in sullen solitude.

Fear of loss had been a potent catalyst for the marriage in the first place, when the dread of rupture through separation that haunted my early childhood had re-emerged soon after I left Yoli in London to attend university in Madrid all those years before. As this fear had gradually receded over time, so too did my perception of the significance of the marriage itself. When it began to happen, I could simply have strayed into a distracting intimacy with others, sexual and otherwise, as many people do with varying degrees of discretion. But such a possibility was too complex and conflicted for my crude emotional puritanism. Instead, I engineered a *separation*, because I felt that by giving it a name and a formally declared status I would somehow have a clearer licence to indulge myself in guilt-free catharsis. I had once walked out of our house in London after an argument and spent the night at the Portobello Hotel, around the corner from the Virgin office. For a few years the hotel would routinely send me a Christmas card thanking me for my custom, and the card's arrival, barely noticed by me, invariably upset Yoli, in whom it prompted a reminder of our increasingly vulnerable state.

On this particular night – having announced that I was packing a bag and leaving – I took a room at the Columbia, a hotel in Lancaster Gate noted for its unblinking, long-suffering approach towards the profligate behaviour of the more badly behaved bands of the period, and therefore frequently patronised by Virgin Records. Anticipating at least some bacchanalian liveliness in the corridors, the place turned out to be sepulchrally quiet, reinforcing my immobilised bewilderment at the extremity of what I had just done. If isolation had a sound, it was the only one I could hear, amplified to a deafening volume.

For a few days I stayed with friends whose marriages were more stable than mine. I went with my children to see films at the weekend, but had no home to take them to afterwards, so spent a great deal of time with them in cafes, striving to avoid tearful scenes by first suppressing my own. On several nights, I slept on a leather sofa in my new office. My ancient dysfunctional dark-green Mercedes saloon, with its ugly tow bar and suscep-tibility to overheated radiator breakdowns, was mostly immobile outside, under the graffiti decorating the boldly art-directed new Virgin office that occupied most of a block on Ladbroke Grove. There were no windows to the front, which instead featured painted *trompe d'oeil* illusions of windows with shattered glass. Spray-painted graffiti usually comes in a wave of monosyllabic abuse, but instead what was spread across the entire front of the building, including the entrance door, was a witheringly concise and considered single-word review of the aesthetics of its attention-seeking design. In large capital letters, it simply read: PRETENTIOUS.

On one of the more distressing nights on the office sofa – quite late and fortified by cheap white wine – I drove to our house in Ealing, let myself in and declared my intention of moving back. There was an ugly stand-off, witnessed by the children, whose pain and incomprehension broke the spell of their parents' rage, prompting us to feel that the only way we might all withstand this dislocating shift in our foundations was to try to perceive it not as rupture but as change, even if the damage already done was irreversible. I visited our home only once more – to collect my belongings, which I did as soon as I had somewhere to put them.

It's axiomatic that a sense of mission can sometimes deflect a sense of loss, particularly when there is constant travel involved. This proved to be the case. During the next weeks, I visited four British cities to promote *Raymond Chandler in Hollywood*, and 19 of them to talk about the two *Yearbooks*. When I returned to London, I moved into an apartment next door to the Townhouse studio in Goldhawk Road, where I had visited numerous recording sessions, including one (XTC's "Roads Girdle the Globe") to which I enthusiastically contributed backing vocals. I had even witnessed a staged arrest there, secretly filmed, of Peter Cook and Dudley Moore while they were making their second Derek and Clive album, with Virgin staff members they didn't recognise disguised as policemen – another of Richard Branson's compulsive, forensically-planned practical jokes. Like the studio, the flat was owned by Virgin and had become vacant exactly when I became homeless, and the studio manager, who lived upstairs, charged me minimal rent until I had my bearings again.

In marrying and fathering so young, I had mostly bypassed adolescence, and the improvisational fearlessness it can engender. At 34, with a broken marriage behind me, it felt a little late to tap into this, but Virgin would have been a good place to do so had I decided to proceed. After a brief period of withdrawal, it was again exploring fresh directions. Salaries remained lower than at comparable organisations, but the reality was that by this stage there were no comparable organisations, and the prospect of a continuing move into film gave it an irresistible extra dimension for me. There were still some subsidiary benefits too, remnants of when the company was relatively small. The Virgin Records weekend away – to which I was still invited, despite the shift of emphasis in my work – was always particularly enjoyable. These company outings began with a 1977 day trip to the Isle of Wight, returning to London by coach in the early hours of the next morning. This had progressed to a riotous weekend in Portugal for the record company's 10th anniversary in 1983, and climaxed for me a year after Richard started his airline, when I hitched a ride with him in an Aztec Piper 6-Seater plane returning from the Lake District so that he could hop off on the runway in London and catch a flight to New York. At the bar and on the dance floor the night before, I had noticed an unfamiliar presence taking an animated interest in befriending the female staff, enjoying numerous cocktails with them well into the early hours. At breakfast later, he was looking a little the worse for wear, his hand shaking perceptibly as he poured the orange juice – as did mine when I realised that he was the pilot of our aircraft and would soon be navigating us through some inevitable turbulence on the flight back to London. We arrived there without incident, his unerring concentration neutralising the toxins coursing through him. Richard left us when we landed and wandered off in the direction of a much larger plane. I don't expect one can any longer drop off a passenger on the tarmac at a British airport, even if he does own an airline.

When *A Shocking Accident* won the Academy Award for best live action short film in 1983 – our modest investment immediately giving us, to our surprise and amusement, a 100% Oscar track record – Richard realised the potential the movie business might have for us, acknowledging that my folly was not entirely without foundation. Within a few months we had three feature films in production. The first was another NFFC/Virgin co-financing collaboration, *Loose Connections*, a romantic comedy directed by Richard Eyre, a distinguished theatre director, whose previous film *The Ploughman's Lunch*, written by Ian McEwan, Virgin was already distributing. (Virgin also distributed films such as the low-budget, pitch-black-funny *Eating Raoul*, directed by Paul Bartel, and featuring himself and longtime friend and frequent co-star, former Warhol acolyte Mary Woronov, in the leading roles.)

For our second and third films, *Secret Places* and *Electric Dreams*, we became a production company. We made the movies, and financed them with other people's money – in the latter case, secured against a "negative pick-up" deal with MGM, which means they had to pay us in full when we delivered the finished film. The directors of these two pictures were mother (Zelda Barron) and son (Steve Barron), each of them well known to us personally and professionally, and both making their first movies. Zelda had worked in various capacities for several notable UK directors (Karel Reisz, Lindsay Anderson, John Boorman, John Schlesinger), and for US actor-producer-directors Warren Beatty (on *Reds*) and Barbra Streisand (on *Yentl*). She was also a fine screenwriter and had adapted Janice Elliott's novel about a young German refugee outsider who arrives at a school in rural England at the beginning of World War 2, and about her friendship with an equally lonely British girl. We were impressed by her script, and believed we could assemble the finance for the low-budget film it would necessarily be, which we did from a number of sources – the NFFC (again), Rank Film Distributors and Rediffusion among them. Zelda had a working relationship with producers Simon Relph and Ann Skinner, whose considerable experience and good judgement strengthened our conviction about her, and although new to the mechanics of filmmaking we felt that if we reinforced Zelda with a strong support team she would rise to the challenge. We did – and so did she. The daughters of familiar and respected actors Maria Schell (Marie-Theres Relin) and Jack MacGowran (Tara MacGowran) played the girls. For the adult roles, I noticed that two actresses I hadn't seen on screen for some time were on the casting director's list, and felt that both would bring some attention to a film with two young unknowns at its centre – Jenny Agutter (spellbinding in *Walkabout*) and Claudine Auger (one of the finest Bond women of all in *Thunderball*). (The following year I came across Claudine at the entrance to the Majestic Hotel in Cannes during the festival. As we stood in front of the hotel – imposingly positioned directly across the road from the Palais des Festivals – we asked each other our business there. I told her I was at the Majestic to meet an American distributor about a film. She told me she was there because her husband owned it.)

Zelda had worked alongside the composer Michel Legrand on *Yentl* and asked if we would approach him to write the score for *Secret Places*. I was an admirer of Legrand, whose contributions to Jacques Demy's two film musicals (*The Umbrellas of Cherbourg* and *The Young Girls of Rochefort*) were extraordinary, as were his scores for *The Thomas Crown Affair* and, particularly, *The*

Go-Between. So I sent him the script, with a note asking him to consider it. He replied immediately after reading. "Count me in on this adventure," he wrote, "I would love to do the music for such a beautiful story." Although I didn't get to know him well, he was one of the most immediately genial and warm-spirited people I met over the numerous years of filmmaking which followed. Later, after seeing a first assembly of the film, he worked out the main theme on the piano, which he played and hummed on a cassette recording and posted it to me to pass on to Zelda. Typically, he prefaced it with perfect brevity and clarity. "'Allo Zelda, it is Michel. I think I have found the music for your wonderful film.'Ere it is…" And so he began.

The advent of MTV in 1981 did not quite invent the pop promo but it dramatically intensified the demand for one to accompany any record that aspired to be a hit. While there was nothing new in having groups lark around in unlikely settings while their songs played – *A Hard Day's Night* comes to mind – the promo liberated pop stars both from the banality of stage performance and from the sheer ordinariness of who they often were. They could reinvent themselves cinematically, tap into their inner actor, control their self-image and, in some cases, travel for fun at someone else's expense to a location not on their touring schedule to shoot it. In their abundance, their ubiquity, their hypnotic repetitiveness, many video clips had their own following. There were even some which people who regularly watched MTV could replicate in their entirety if you just played the recording.

Zelda's son Steve Barron had already made several striking promos for Virgin groups The Human League and Simple Minds, and, beyond Virgin, for the likes of Madonna, Sheena Easton and Spandau Ballet. It was just a matter of when he would make his first film, since studios were by then pursuing the new wave of music video directors, whose style would attract and satisfy the rapidly multiplying young demographic. Like mother Zelda, Steve was "family" at Virgin. The script of *Electric Dreams* – a fantasy comedy MTV would have been proud to come up with itself, about a computer that falls in love with its owner/ programmer's girlfriend – had been written by an American, Rusty Lemorande, who along with his fellow producer Larry DeWaay (and Zelda), had also worked on *Yentl* with Streisand, suggesting that imminent approaches to Virgin Films may have been a recurrent topic of off-camera discussion on that particular set. Lemorande had earlier been hired by Jon Peters as a production executive on the box-office hit *Caddyshack,* and at times appeared to be channelling some of the alpha swagger of his former employer, to whose level of populist success he clearly aspired.

Although interiors were built and shot at Twickenham Studios in London, the exteriors were filmed in San Francisco, where I spent a day on location nursing a 101.4 degree temperature on a cold, blustery, abandoned Alcatraz island. While the film's technology now appears comically primitive, and its level of cuteness overbearing, it turned out to be a good-natured and deftly-executed film, with all the concomitant assets and liabilities of the early-80s MTV aesthetic. We had an outstanding cinematographer (Alex Thomson), production designer (Richard Macdonald) and costume designer (Ruth Myers) – and Lemorande persuaded Bud Cort (Harold in *Harold and Maude*), by now in his mid-30s, to be the voice of the computer, performing his lines live from inside a box in the studio, and never seen on set by the other actors.

The songs – several contributed by frequent MTV presences Boy George and Culture Club, and ELO's Jeff Lynne – were seamlessly integrated into the film, but most effective of all were the opening and closing ones, one by PP Arnold to draw you in, the other by Giorgio Moroder and Philip Oakey of The Human League, to see you out. When I first heard the latter – on my car cassette player, driving an American friend on a sunny Saturday morning from Gatwick airport to a cross-channel ferry in Newhaven – I had to stop by the side of the road. I was evidently unable to drive and be overwhelmed at the same time, as there were two other occasions I was compelled to do this during the period in question – with Michel Legrand's voice-and-piano sketch for *Secret Places* and David Bowie's demo of the *Absolute Beginners* title song. More about the latter later.

Visits to Hollywood around this time were increasingly enjoyable. Because various distribution rights to *Electric Dreams*, including the US, had been pre-bought by MGM, we were regally entertained in the studio commissary by studio head Frank Yablans, with numerous people – including one of my heroes, *Big Wednesday* writer-director and *Apocalypse Now* co-writer John Milius, then shooting *Red Dawn* on the lot – dropping by to greet us. And Larry Schiller, the producer-director of the Norman Mailer-scripted *The Executioner's Song*, which Virgin distributed theatrically in the UK, threw us a small drinks party at which the guest of honour was one of the film's stars Rosanna Arquette, on whom, unable to conceal my inner schoolboy, I had a fleeting crush. And, as only a film-geek would, I also wasted social opportunities in this first flush of attention because when Columbia asked me what they could offer me on the lot that they could reasonably provide, I nominated a screening of a rare print of their 1967 film *The Love-Ins*, in which Richard Todd, only 12 years after famously portraying World War 2 air force hero Guy Gibson in *The Dam Busters*, improbably represents a messianic, drug-advocating college professor modelled on Timothy Leary.

Back in London, because we distributed films in the UK – as well as developing, financing and producing them – I received calls from practically everybody who was making or selling a film that was not studio-financed. One was from a sales agent called Omar Kaczmarczyk – unbelievably, considering his line of work, his surname was pronounced "Cashmacheque", something he took as much pleasure in declaring as we did in joking about it. I had first encountered him at the Cannes Film Festival, where Alexander and Ilya Salkind, the successful independent producers whose films he represented, had a splashy, self-aggrandising annual ritual. One lunchtime at the peak of the festival, a group of small planes from the nearby air base would fly in formation at very low altitude past the beaches – where Cannes delegates would be tucking into their *salades niçoises* and cold *rosé* under the Riviera sun – announcing their productions. These had included *Superman, Superman 2, Superman 3* and, most recently, *Supergirl*, which was still filming when I first witnessed the event. The element which gave it a stunt-like precision specific to their environment, and which added to the amusement, was that these planes flew their banners in a configuration exactly reflecting the contractual billing of these films, with the presentation credit being towed by the top plane and "directed by" by the lowest. I always felt that the joke was missing a punchline – a tiny aircraft, flying under all the others and slightly lagging, dragging a little banner that read "credits not contractual", the maxim added at the bottom of announcement ads for films still in production or negotiation. The Salkinds were the lords of Cannes before Menahem Golan of Cannon, then Harvey Weinstein of Miramax, succeeded them, and the annual flypast was a signature flourish, simply because they could. Reflecting both their grandeur and their independence, their films were for the most part financed through pre-sales to distributors, which is perhaps one of the reasons they were so wealthy.

Omar called me one day from the Dorchester Hotel, where he appeared to be sharing a suite with the script of *Santa Claus – the Movie*, as there was nobody else there and he referred to it so often. Since the Superman films had been directed by Richards Donner and Lester, I had thought one of them, both fine directors, might have the right touch of mischief to bring to life something which could potentially lapse into fatal whimsy. However, Omar told me the director was to be Jeannot Szwarc, who would start filming this immediately after completing *Supergirl*. The script was so coveted, so secret and so protected, that he was inviting me to come over and read it in his suite at the Dorchester. This was a novel strategy I hadn't encountered before, and I was curious to see where it might lead. When I arrived there, he went a stage further: he would read it *to* me, he said. Since I hadn't had anything read to me since I was a small child, I suggested I take the script into another room and read it myself. One could see the spectres of small spy cameras and photographic memories cross his eyes. Sorry, he said – he couldn't risk it, he would have to read it to me.

So he did. His pitch would go UP when he was playing an elf or some other small, playful character, or DOWN if he was being Santa himself, or anyone else who might be old and bearded. Female characters had a daintier cadence in the delivery, as if they had all stepped out of a fairytale – as I suppose they had. Dudley Moore was to play the star elf, Patch, but nobody else had yet been cast. Occasionally there might be a brief interruption to the reading as a new pot of tea in Dorchester silverware was delivered to the suite to sustain Omar, or another tray of cucumber sandwiches to suppress my disbelief. Never, surely, has such a lacklustre script been performed with such remarkable conviction by the person trying to sell it.

Improbable experiences with film people in expensive London hotels aside (another involved a visit to Elliott Gould at the Inn on the Park, his room window wide open at his insistence as a freezing gale blew in from Hyde Park across the road) – and with *Secret Places* and *Electric Dreams* by then both in post-production – most of our attention was on finding a project we wanted to make in 1984. Through Virgin's financing and distribution involvement in *Loose Connections*, I knew the producer Simon Perry quite well, and had admired *Another Time, Another Place*, his collaboration with writer-director Michael Radford, so I was intrigued by what the two of them would do next.

A few years earlier a Chicago lawyer called Marvin Rosenblum had noted the accelerating proximity of 1984 in his calendar and flown to London to persuade George Orwell's widow Sonia to sell him the film rights to Orwell's book *Nineteen Eighty-Four* (the correct title is spelt out), of which there had been two lacklustre adaptations in the mid-1950s, now long out of circulation. Before travelling to see her, he studied Orwell's work with great thoroughness, as if preparing a case. Impressed by his enthusiasm and erudition, Mrs Orwell agreed to his offer, then died a few days later. Now, in the late autumn of 1983, time was again running out if *Nineteen Eighty-Four* were to come out in the year of its title. Rosenblum's attempt at a script – written by Paul Mayersberg, with whom I was soon to make another quite different film – airlifted the book's dystopian universe to the US in the unspecified future. The project's scale dictated studio finance and none of them, intimidated by its bleakness, were interested.

Unaware of this history, Radford was himself sufficiently curious about the book to have made his own enquiries about the rights, a path which led to Rosenblum, from whom one night he received a phone call from Chicago. It didn't require a sophisticated movie brain to conclude that, if the film were to open in October 1984, it would need to start shooting around mid-March, finish no later than mid-to-late June, and have no more than three months to complete all post-production for a world premiere in early-to-mid October. In three weeks, Radford wrote a script. Respectful of the book, its ingenious foundation stone for the film's look and feel was the idea that Orwell, who wrote the book in 1948, had simply flipped the 8 and 4 for its title, and that instead of showing some imagined future world the film would reveal one in which every building, object, surface and texture was suspended and frozen in 1948.

The prospect of financing, preparing, shooting, completing and releasing *Nineteen Eighty-Four*, all within its eponymous year, was irresistible to people like us, for whom a challenge and a sense of event were factors which determined so many decisions. So, when Radford and Perry came to Virgin – aware that it was their final shot at making the film in the time frame, and that this could be made to work *only* if the budget could be raised within a month, and that the month in question was January when money people take winter holidays – we decided to go ahead regardless and commit the first budget guesstimate of £2.5m. We could bring in other financiers if and required.

Or so we thought.

CHAPTER TWELVE

When the making of a film is locked into as rigid a completion date as *Nineteen Eighty-Four*'s was, it both simplifies and complicates casting. It simplifies because it focuses the attention entirely on considerations of aptitude, affordability, availability and commercial viability. It complicates because you can't wait for anyone, however right for the role, who vacillates for long or is already committed to another project during the required period. Establishing and eliminating possibilities as rapidly as possible is a crucial fundamental in not running the risk of being left stranded.

Casting the lead role of Winston Smith was textbook-straightforward. Radford approached John Hurt at an industry gathering, asked him if he would do it, and Hurt said yes. Identifying a Julia, the young woman with whom Smith becomes perilously involved, was a little more complicated. Jenny Seagrove – who had recently played dreamy *ingénues* in both *A Shocking Accident* and *Local Hero* – was suggested but was resistant to the nudity required. My colleague Robert Devereux had recently seen Jamie Lee Curtis in *Trading Places* and became taken with the idea of casting her as Julia – it would certainly have helped the film's American profile – while Radford favoured Suzanna Hamilton, whose elusive amalgam of wistful idealism and conniving knowingness ended up being perfect for the role. She had also recently appeared naked in the film adaptation of Dennis Potter's *Brimstone and Treacle*, so was unintimidated by the required on-screen nudity.

Two months before the start of shooting, whose schedule would reflect the same months Orwell describes in the book, we had not yet cast the imposing inquisitor and torturer O'Brien, a role requiring a well-known middle-aged male star of authority and charisma who might compensate for the fact that Hurt and Hamilton would not generate commercial confidence on their own. Nor, more immediately, would they attract the US distributor we were seeking in order to diminish our considerable risk, particularly as the first real budget, at £3.7m, was rather more than the back-of-an-envelope estimate on which we had entered the arena. For this amount, we needed a safety net. The company's adventurous spirit, its flair for risk-taking improvisation and its ability to make and implement decisions quickly – qualities on which Virgin was built – were being put to the test in an exacting way.

Radford flew to Málaga to visit Sean Connery at his home in Marbella, near the golf course where he spent much of his time between films. He had recently made a perfunctory return to the screen as James Bond in the "unofficial" Bond movie *Never Say Never Again*, a barely disguised remake of *Thunderball* from 18 years earlier, its title a winking allusion to a statement Connery had once made about never playing Bond again after he had finished *Diamonds Are Forever*. (Many years later, Daniel Craig also said "never" after *Spectre* before being lured back for *No Time to Die* by the usual method – money.) Disregarding our obvious urgency, Connery dithered for a month then declined, opting instead to play a Spanish swordsman called Ramirez (with the Scots accent he routinely applied to all nationalities) who tutors Christopher Lambert in *Highlander*. We then asked Paul Scofield – an Oscar winner for *A Man for All Seasons* – but he had broken his leg and would be immobilised for some time. Then there was Rod Steiger, who after a series of tragicomic telex misunderstandings concerning a non-existent wife, turned out to be in hospital and not available. We discussed Gene Hackman, Anthony Hopkins, Jason Robards – each of whom might have been perfect in the role – but none of them materialised.

Holding our nerve, re-scheduling the O'Brien scenes to as late as possible in the shoot, and three weeks away from the start of principal photography, we attempted to find a US distributor during the American Film Market in Los Angeles. Despite the novel's iconographic status and the fact that it was then selling around 10,000 copies a week in the US, there was resistance. With the exception of Disney, I think we tried everyone: Frank Yablans at MGM, Michael Eisner at Paramount, Mark Rosenberg at Warner, Mike Medavoy at Orion, Bob Bookman at Columbia, Sean Daniel at Universal, Joe Wizan at Fox, Craig Baumgarten at Lorimar. Perhaps they considered Virgin to be wealthy dilettantes because Richard Branson was about to launch his own airline and none of them were. In any event, it was clear they believed that we needed them more than they did us, since we were in a hurry and they weren't. It didn't help that the advance word on *Electric Dreams* was discouraging, compounded when it later opened to mediocre box office. Convincing a studio to take on *Nineteen Eighty-Four* was as frustrating an obstacle for us as it was a problem for them: a difficult sell to an American audience, confronting and tragic, and without a Robert De Niro or a Jack Nicholson to give it Oscar lustre. Or perhaps it was simply our outsider status which prompted suspicion. As Fox head Darryl Zanuck remarked of the revered French director Jean Renoir during the latter's years in Hollywood in the 1940s, "Jean Renoir is a great artist, but he's not one of us."

Nevertheless, if a company was perceived to have money and a modicum of taste, as Virgin did, you certainly got to meet interesting people. One day I was dropping off a tape at home to Barbra Streisand, whom we had invited to sing Alan Jay Lerner's lyrics for Michel Legrand's main theme for *Secret Places* – eventually recorded by Kiri Te Kanawa instead – and the next we were having lunch with Orson Welles at the fabled Ma Maison, still vibrant but undeniably in decline. He lunched there every day. They even took his mail and phone calls. (It was to close 18 months later, three weeks after Welles's death, restaurant and favoured customer in a nearly synchronised final curtain.) Although a large man for much of his adult life, Welles was enormous by this stage and moved with great difficulty, so his table was positioned near the door to the parking lot, eliminating the need for him to navigate the restaurant space at all since he could just slip in and out. He was a charismatic, eloquent and practised lunch companion, seamlessly navigating us through his proposed adaptation of *King Lear* (to be financed by French television, which later withdrew), his script of Isaac Dinesen's *The Dreamers*, his long unfinished film *The Other Side of the Wind* – which financing from Netflix would pay to complete and release 34 years later – and his most recent screenplay, *The Big Brass Ring*, a political drama eventually directed by the improbably named George Hickenlooper in 1999 after re-writing Welles's and Oja Kodar's script.

The problem was that by this stage Virgin had so much riding on *Nineteen Eighty-Four* that, although we continued to develop projects, we couldn't realistically consider fully financing another film until this one was completed and sold. The difficulty had not diminished when I returned to London and went to Claridges to meet Martin Scorsese, trying to raise finance for *The Last Temptation of Christ*, which had run its course at Paramount, and he was now attempting to set up independently. At this time, Aidan Quinn was to play Jesus, with Sting as Pontius Pilate and

Barbara Hershey as Mary Magdalene. It was a tantalising prospect to work with this virtuoso cine-literate director – one comparable in his idiosyncratic flair and ambition to Welles in some respects, but also one whose most recent film, *The King of Comedy*, had been a notable commercial failure.

Scorsese's then chronic allergy to smoke (despite the tremendous amount of smoking in most of his movies) promised a repeat of Elliott Gould's hotel moment with the open windows and the howling gale, so I resisted firing up a cigarette during our long encounter. I was familiar with his idiosyncrasies through a friend who had worked for him and De Niro on *Raging Bull*. One of them was that he spoke very quickly. As with Welles, it was frustrating not to be able to take the conversation further, especially with a film which promised such controversy, to whose seductive allure we were invariably drawn as a company. However, by making *After Hours* and *The Color of Money* in the two years that followed – one a masterfully contained and orchestrated low-budget black comedy, the other a sequel propelled by two charismatic stars a generation apart – Scorsese made himself bankable again, with Universal wholly financing *Last Temptation*, now with Willem Dafoe as Jesus, David Bowie as Pontius Pilate and Barbara Hershey – still – as Mary Magdalene. (The film's subject alone guaranteed its notoriety, with the anticipated hostile displays materialising in several of the countries it played in, including an unusual one in Australia: outside its Sydney premiere, among the usual demonstrators, was a breakaway group, evidently devotees of *Monty Python's Life of Brian*, protesting that the film had failed to acknowledge Brian as the true Messiah.)

In the meantime, the screenplay of *Nineteen Eighty-Four* had been sent to Richard Burton, of whom none of us had thought earlier. He was said to be in Haiti at the time, not a location one would then have associated with the rapid delivery of urgent scripts, so we were relieved when he promptly agreed to do it. Although Burton's career had been in gradual decline since the late 1960s, with his seven Oscar nominations as best actor he remained without question the movie star the film did not yet have. His oratorial voice, as unmistakable as Welles's, was put to unexpectedly effective use by simply turning down the dial. Since it is the intimacy he establishes with Smith – even when torturing him – that gives their scenes a compelling stillness, Radford encouraged Burton to speak with a kind of muted fondness, his voice a beguiling lethal weapon. The unanticipated liability was the length of these speeches, which after many years of hard living he found difficult to remember, requiring multiple takes. At the end of a particularly difficult day, with an exhausted Burton already on his way back to his lodgings, Radford was unable to conceal his exasperation. "The trouble," he exclaimed, "is that his brain is so full of Shakespearean speeches and theatre stories that there's *no room for my script!*"

We had earlier announced Burton's casting at a breakfast we held at the Cannes Film Festival. It was the only year that Virgin rented a yacht from which to operate, and it was a disaster. We lived on it, which saved on hotel accommodation costs, and the idea was to invite distributors from around the world in various configurations to lunch on the deck with us. Every day it poured with rain, each a little more than the day before. Cannes loses all its lustre in the wet. Small yachts are cold and restrictive when you're confined inside, so each lunchtime we escorted the distributors to a series of restaurants on the adjacent harbourside, all of them profiting from our predicament. Thankfully, the deals compensated for the meals. We sold territories – but still not the US.

On return, I received a visit from Simon Perry, the producer Virgin had entrusted with its millions. He had already worked effectively with us before, but it was evident that he was in a state of shock. The film was going well in many respects, he prefaced, but there was one in which it wasn't. It would be substantially over budget: more than £1 million over. He took responsibility and accepted fault, but essentially blamed the production manager he had employed and the accountant that came with him, for a serious miscalculation. It was a more complicated film than the original budget reflected, he said, and its time-consuming size and complexity had prevented him from checking the escalating costs with the frequency and precision he should have. Richard Branson was staggered, for a moment speechless, but surprisingly sanguine. He was about to launch a transatlantic airline at considerable financial risk, a venture put together at breakneck speed, so this was not something he wanted to hear. However, with Phil Collins, Culture Club, The Human League, Heaven 17 and Simple Minds, among others, Virgin had enjoyed a remarkable couple of years of growth and success, and the film was now pre-sold to many territories, so the film's overage, while an extremely unwelcome surprise, was not going to paralyse us. Fundamentally, we had a choice between continuing to finance the film or closing it down, which by then was no choice at all.

But it did mean many visits to Twickenham Studios, visits I wish I had made more frequently and more rigorously earlier in the process. The parts of the film not shot there were filmed on various locations – the burnt-out shell of Alexandra Palace for Victory Square; Wiltshire for the country idyll and the aircraft hangar used in the opening scene; Senate House for the Ministry of Truth; Battersea Power Station; a Shoreditch street; but primarily at the disused and abandoned Beckton gas works in

East London, a perfect dystopian setting around which surveillance helicopters could be flown close to buildings. It was a place with which one could take so many liberties that Stanley Kubrick subsequently followed us in to film the second half of *Full Metal Jacket*. He stuck up a few palm trees and turned it into Vietnam, not long before the area was scheduled for complete demolition, something he was clearly happy to help on its way. Terry Gilliam was making *Brazil* – also set in a malign universe of the imagination – at the same time as us, so there were unavoidable overlaps and collisions.

The budget blow-out increased pressure on the film to perform on a mainstream scale. Once it had finished shooting – a week over schedule – we concluded that this could only come in the form of a score and corresponding soundtrack album that might have a successful life of its own. The composer Dominic Muldowney had already written a majestic "Oceania" anthem for the main title sequence and elsewhere, in the rousing melodic spirit of Ennio Morricone's *1900* theme, but it required something more commercially exploitable to add another dimension to our chances of recoupment.

A few days after we finished filming, Richard Branson, Mike Radford and I had lunch with David Bowie on Richard's houseboat. Bowie had just returned from Quebec, where he had been working on an album, *Tonight*, with producer Hugh Padgham, whom we knew well from his work on Phil Collins, Peter Gabriel and XTC albums, all recorded at the Townhouse. We were very much aware of Bowie's songs "1984" and "Big Brother" on his *Diamond Dogs* album and his once-declared intention, rejected by Orwell's widow Sonia, of creating and performing an entire musical inspired by the novel. On every level, he seemed the perfect first choice. He brought along his son, a very well-behaved 13-year-old introduced as Joe – later to become the film director Duncan Jones – who quietly sat out on the canal towpath reading a book. Although attentive and focused, Bowie had a playful air about him, a sense of mischief, and he and Radford seemed to get along well. I remember a journalist's later account of interviewing Bowie in a hotel room somewhere. She had arrived with a long list of prepared questions in a notebook but found herself so entertained that she never referred to them. Back in the lobby after the interview's conclusion, she realised she had left the notebook behind, called up to the room, went back to collect it, and knocked. The door was opened by a smiling Bowie, who as he handed it to her simply said: "You'll never know".

His musical ideas for the film, however, sounded quite abstract, the cost of his involvement prohibitive, and his timetable too congested. So, we asked Peter Gabriel, who was unavailable. Then the Eurythmics, who were in the Bahamas. Despite the chronic urgency, they were keen to attempt it and were sent a video of an advanced picture cut. Radford had various phone conversations with them, was clearly doubtful it could be made to work, but agreed to listen with as open a mind as he could manage.

At the beginning of August – shortly after completing his post-synching and exactly two months before the UK opening of the film – Richard Burton died of a brain haemorrhage in Switzerland. A few weeks later there was a memorial service at St Martin-in-the-Fields in Trafalgar Square, attended by three of his wives – Sally, to whom he was married at the time; Suzy Hunt, to whom he was married before that; and Elizabeth Taylor, to whom he was (twice) married most famously of all. Police had some trouble keeping the traffic moving in the celebrity congestion in this busiest of thoroughfares.

As we prepared for the October 7 world premiere, there was a phone call from Valerie Douglas, Burton's business manager, who had heard that we might be inviting Taylor to it. His wife Sally, she told me, was still reeling from the humiliation of the memorial service, at which she was seated with Burton's friends and acquaintances while Elizabeth Taylor, an ex-wife twice removed, was with his family. Taylor, she said, was "a travelling circus, a one-woman riot" who posed numerous problems. She would require considerable security as she attracted all kinds of crazies, and had a sizeable entourage, whose bills she would expect paid. Her presence, Douglas believed, would make people feel that the film needed her as a "publicity crutch", whereas Sally would actually promote it by attending the press lunch and doing interviews on behalf of her late husband.

The premiere, not attended by Elizabeth Taylor, was a great success. Although everybody acknowledged that it was a remarkable achievement to have made the journey from nothing to premiere on a film of this scale and ambition in well under a year, it was important that it should have a powerful critical and commercial impact. It did. The reviews were unswervingly positive – praising the fidelity to the book, the vitality of the filmmaking, the authenticity of its performances, and the extraordinary cinematography by Roger Deakins – and the movie broke attendance records in London in its first week. It had, however, opened without the Eurythmics part of the music score, since there had only been a few days to begin integrating it into the Dominic Muldowney score, already recorded as a safety measure. Initially, the two scores did sit a little strangely together, but this didn't diminish the film in any way, and it was an important commercial protection for Virgin. When the tidal wave of critical approval for the film kicked in, increased resistance from Radford and Perry to the proposed music changes did too, although the work was finally accomplished. Not content with winning best film and best actor (John Hurt) awards at the Standard Film Awards a month later, Radford was unable to resist some self-righteous sabotage by emphasising his displeasure in his acceptance speech, this despite the film's continuing success, with substantial openings and capacity business in Germany, France, Scandinavia and Australia. It was a difficult time for us all, each operating from a complicated mix of pragmatism and self-interest, always feeling that justice favoured us.

In the meantime, we had finally succeeded in securing US distribution with Atlantic Releasing, a company which had begun life in edgy auteur arthouse fare (Dusan Makavejev's *Montenegro*, Kathryn Bigelow's debut *The Loveless*) and was now, buoyed by the confidence of a trio of successful wide-release performers (*Teen Wolf*, *Valley Girl*, *Night of the Comet*), seeking to combine prestige and commerciality. They orchestrated a terrific campaign at remarkable speed – a week-long engagement from December 12 at the Egyptian in Westwood as an Oscar-qualifying run, reinforced with a double-page ad in *Variety* and an excellent *Los Angeles Times* review on opening day. I travelled over to visit them and witness all this. One evening, I drove past a long line of people outside the cinema on Wilshire Boulevard queuing to get into the film, then went on to a screening at the Academy of Motion Picture Arts and Sciences, where I sat nervously outside the door, anticipating, then witnessing, the walkouts during the torture scene. In one bleakly comic moment, an older woman paused on the threshold of an exit she had pushed open and announced, "I feel nauseous!", before stumbling into the lobby.

Divisive as it was in its extremes, *Nineteen Eighty-Four* was a success in the US, its box office of $8.5m a strong result at the time for an uncompromising independent British movie opening against the tide during the festive season. It was also a hit in a number of other major territories, and in the course of its release Virgin sold 100,000 Eurythmics' soundtrack albums and 200,000 copies of the single "Sexcrime", taken from it, in the UK alone.

A few months later, Mike Radford and I resumed what had once been an agreeable relationship before it was interrupted by the fractures that followed the conflict over music. We were at the Istanbul Film Festival, to which the film had been invited. Two screenings had been arranged, scheduled three hours apart. At the first – in a bizarre presentation more befitting an opera diva – each of us was given an enormous bunch of flowers and asked to bring them back so they could be presented to us again at the second screening. So, we took the flowers to a bar where we sat in a big booth, two oversized bunches of blooms occupying the space between us.

Over 70 years after publication, the contemporary resonances of *Nineteen Eighty-Four* – and George Orwell's prescience in creating the world within it – remain remarkable. When, in an early 2017 statement, Donald Trump's then senior adviser Kellyanne Conway referred to "alternative facts", it sounded unmistakably like *newspeak*, the obfuscatory language of Oceania intended to confuse and conceal that is introduced by Orwell as an inherent part of his society. Soon after she used this term, sales of the book increased by 9,500%, a best seller again in the 21st century, and forever.

CHAPTER THIRTEEN

1984 was a year so engulfing that in the course of it part of me went into a desensitised dream state, responding to events in my personal life in watchful objectivity, aware of their significance yet somehow despatching them to the margins.

At the beginning of it, I moved to a modest walk-up third-storey apartment into which I delusionally thought I could fit a large jukebox, and I succeeded in visiting the nearby hospital's casualty department on three occasions in the same month, unrelated except in my sudden talent for misfortune – with a fishbone lodged in my throat, with blood pouring out of my right index finger after an incident involving a tin of corned beef, and finally with grit grinding across the cornea of one of my eyes after a run on a dusty, blustery evening.

Towards the end of it, my ex-wife Yoli, having re-married shortly after our divorce was finalised, gave birth to her daughter Isabella, and my mother was admitted to a hospital an hour's drive inland from the Scottish seaside town of Ardrossan – to which she and my father had retired some years earlier – diagnosed with liver cancer. She rallied a little with cortisone treatment, but as its palliative effectiveness diminished it became only a matter of time. I saw my children at weekends, and did my best to be a loving father, if also a distracted one.

During it, *Secret Places* was released to admiring reviews and respectable returns – a gentle, precision-tuned and well-received film which declared us to be a fully functional production company. "Magically exact", "accomplished and affecting", "I was moved, amused and enthralled" were among the British print media responses. Later, in America, it was even better. Rex Reed of the *New York Post* wrote of it as "a miracle... sensitive, beautifully acted, riveting and disturbing", and Kathleen Carroll of the *New York Daily News* called it "a poignant bittersweet movie". And although too stretched financially to bankroll another film during the rest of a year monopolised by *Nineteen Eighty-Four*, we could still develop projects towards turning them into something worth making – and we did.

One of them began life as a 12-page treatment called *Rights* by Paul Mayersberg, equal parts extended synopsis and absorbing self-interrogation. Mayersberg had worked for producer-director Roger Corman in the 1960s, contributing uncredited script work and second unit directing to Corman's film *The Tomb of Ligeia*, before writing the remarkable screenplays of *The Man Who Fell to Earth* and *Eureka* for Nicolas Roeg. He now wanted to direct a film built from an idea of his own – loosely inspired by events surrounding the case of kidnapped heiress Patty Hearst – both of us unaware at this stage that the title *Rights* would change to *Heroine* before production and, finally, in response to distributor resistance after completion, to *Captive*.

The second project was *Castaway*, an adaptation of the Lucy Irvine book, which I wanted Roeg to direct. Indeed, it was only of interest to me if he did. I had been spellbound by all of his seven films to date and was certain he could bring depth, drama, humour, beauty, even mystery, to what might in other hands have been simply a behavioural two-hander about an ill-matched man and woman on a desert island. His *Eureka* producer Jeremy Thomas had asked me a few years earlier to organise a DJ for the film's end-of-shoot party. My reward was to be invited to a gathering at which I knew no one but witnessed everything, enjoying in particular the perceptible rise in room temperature on the arrival of Roeg's wife and muse Theresa Russell, golden-haired and caramel-tanned in a green dress that clung to every contour. Allan Scott – who had written the screenplay for Roeg's earlier, extraordinary *Don't Look Now* – was soon engaged to adapt Irvine's book, so following show business custom we celebrated with a lively lunch. Like most such occasions, it was premature in its optimism. (The project's eventual move to Cannon Films – after nearly a year of planning, casting and crewing – was prompted primarily by the fact that it couldn't be made for the agreed budget, which we were not prepared to increase. For his location, Roeg chose Aitutaki in the Cook Islands, in the middle of the South Pacific. Tim Van Rellim – the production manager who followed him there and had worked with him a few years earlier on *Bad Timing* – summarised the problem succinctly in a telex. All it said was: "We'll have to fly in every toothpick". To no one's surprise, the film was later relocated to the Seychelles, exactly half the distance from London.)

Completing the trio of single-word titles was *Gothic*, a script by Stephen Volk which took a summer spent in a villa on the banks of Lake Leman in Switzerland by Byron, Shelley, Shelley's wife Mary, Mary's stepsister Claire Clairmont and Byron's friend Dr Polidori, and condensed it into a single hallucinatory night of ghost stories, seances laced with opium and laudanum, and a storm raging outside, inspiring Mary Shelley to write her seminal novel *Frankenstein*, and Dr Polidori *The Vampyre*, a precursor to *Dracula*. We had yet to choose a director for it but were confident that the extreme nature of the material itself would attract the right one.

And then there was Jim Steinman. Channelling the colliding musical spirits of Richard Wagner and Phil Spector – reinforced with compelling stadium-rock air-punching choruses – Steinman had written Meat Loaf's *Bat Out of Hell* album nearly a decade earlier, then struggled to find a company to release it. When one finally did so, it became a massive success, along with the singles taken from it. Steinman was not shy about embracing the grandiose, but his approach was also playful, spirited and fresh, one of its identifying features being the lengthy, often parenthesised titles of many of his songs, which one suspected had actually begun life as titles. Among them were "Good Girls Go to Heaven (Bad Girls Go Everywhere)", "I'd Do Anything for Love (But I Won't Do That)", "You Took the Words Right Out of My Mouth" and, most memorable of all, "Loving You's a Dirty Job (But Somebody's Gotta Do It)".

By the time we met, his best-known song was "Total Eclipse of the Heart", the mega-ballad recorded by Bonnie Tyler in 1983. Consonant with my title-comes-first speculation, Steinman now wanted to turn that title into a film. And reflecting the song's scale and ambition, his idea was a contemporary variation on *Wuthering Heights* set in the vineyards north of San Francisco, with Heathcliff as a kind of Jim Morrison/Michael Hutchence-like figure, moodily picking grapes shirtless – but not singing – while Cathy was the romantically-awakened manor girl yearning for him as she strolled dreamily past the vines. The scriptwriter Steinman had in mind was Patricia Louisianna Knop, who with her husband Zalman King had written the screenplay *9½ Weeks*, and so had already shown her skill in walking the tightrope while also pushing the envelope, as it were. Would we be interested in developing the script, attracting a mutually agreed director, and putting together the finance?

At dinner together in a restaurant around the corner from the Virgin office, we wasted little time examining the menu. Instead,

Steinman did something I had never witnessed before, reflecting the strangely sheltered life I had led over a period in which the music business's high-life practices had intensified but somehow bypassed me: he ordered every single appetiser on the menu, and worked his way through them as our conversation progressed. Afterwards, I drove him back to his hotel at Marble Arch, and in the car began playing him an advance cassette of Frankie Goes To Hollywood's first album which I had received earlier that day. The group were at their peak commercially, several advance singles from the LP had already been hits, and I thought that Steinman would enjoy their music's vigour and density, and Trevor Horn's epic production. We travelled in attentive, expectant silence. After a lengthy instrumental intro to the title track, the first lyrics kicked in – "In Xanadu did Kubla Khan a stately pleasure dome decree…" I looked over to Steinman, rolling his eyes in disbelief at the opening line he had just heard. "And they call ME pretentious!" he scoffed.

Like Steinman, I was predisposed to songs with elaborate titles, most of which lived up to their promise, and were often unusual portraits of solitude, anger and loss. My favourites included "If You Leave Me, Can I Come Too?" by the Australian group Mental as Anything, Kevin Ayers' "Diminished But Not Finished", Mayday Parade's "If You Can't Live Without Me, Why Aren't You Dead Yet?", Warren Zevon's "If You Won't Leave Me, I'll Find Somebody Who Will" and – country music providing reliably fertile ground for such emotional warfare – "She Got the Gold Mine, and I Got the Shaft" by Jerry Reed. There were also some which weren't acrimonious love songs at all, more declarations of intent: "I'd Rather Have a Bottle in Front of Me (Than a Frontal Lobotomy)" by Dr Rock (aka Randy Hazlitt) comes to mind. And later, in the realm of unanticipated puns, it would be difficult to eclipse Squeeze singer-songwriter Chris Difford's title for his 2008 solo album, *The Last Temptation of Chris*.

But what had occupied much of our planning attention during the preceding year – sometimes as if it were a film already in production (as *Nineteen Eighty-Four* had actually been at the time) rather than an ambitious project we were still developing – was *Absolute Beginners*. Based on Colin MacInnes's novel – written in 1958, published the following year – it began as a persuasive monologue in my office from Julien Temple, whom I knew from his involvement with the Sex Pistols, their videos and the film *The Great Rock'n'Roll Swindle*. His pitch was that, in the book's account of Soho in that era, MacInnes emphasised how much this vibrant melting pot of central London was propelled by jazz, and by the beginnings of a teenage aesthetic, as the city emerged from its dreary monochrome post-war lethargy. Add to this the cultural shift then under way through the rising numbers of West Indian migrants settling in the Notting Hill area, and there was a social backdrop against which these musical sequences could play and be enriched. In effect, he would reshape the novel into a screen musical, a jazz musical, with dance numbers and visual flourishes worthy of vintage Vincente Minnelli or Stanley Donen. Young men and women were playing and listening to jazz again, he said, and there was a new jazz emerging out of this. He would invite me to the Electric Ballroom in Camden Town to witness it one night – and quite lively it was, with enough mid-80s cool posturing in lightweight suits to make it seem of the moment. That's what we were seeking – time-specific and timeless at the same time.

Each month, more people seemed to be fluctuating in the mix, and higher estimates added to the budget. Temple's friend and colleague (and later mine) Michael Hamlyn, with whom he had been developing the project so far, gave way as producer to Steve Woolley, Chris Brown and Nik Powell at Palace, to us at Virgin (where Nik had, of course, once been Richard's business partner), and then to Goldcrest, who were planning to embark on an expensive trio of films. While we were having problems with the escalating cost of *Nineteen Eighty-Four*, Goldcrest would eventually have theirs with *Revolution*. The scale and objective of such films (and their corresponding budget increases) tended to grow daily once under way, and we needed more preparation time to guard against this happening with *Absolute Beginners*, as expenditure rose and musical horizons expanded. The legendary arranger of Miles Davis's pioneering, era-defining late 50s recordings, Gil Evans, would supervise the music. And we agreed that we would need to build the world of the film on a studio stage, since most of it didn't exist anymore, certainly not in a way that was accessible and controllable.

There were days when I attended a *Nineteen Eighty-Four* cost report meeting at Twickenham Studios that ran for most of the morning, then moved on to an *Absolute Beginners* script discussion at Goldcrest's offices which would go on from mid-afternoon into the evening, once ending eight hours later after a long argumentative dinner. It was comforting to be in league with Goldcrest, an experienced film company with a solid track record, whose head of production Sandy Lieberson I knew and liked and trusted. Virgin's 50% contribution to the budget of *Absolute Beginners* also secured us soundtrack rights, and we were confident that these would generate considerable income to offset potential losses on the film itself. Like *Nineteen Eighty-Four*, the picture was certain to be so high-profile as to be unavoidable, but this time we would not be the only vulnerable party, particularly as no US distribution was in prospect until Temple and Woolley

– via an introduction from Bob Dylan's then-lawyer, with whom Temple was discussing work – convinced Mike Medavoy at Orion to take it on.

And so began 1985. Four months ahead of our scheduled shoot start, we built an elaborate set and filmed a scene at Twickenham Studios to satisfy a request from Orion, who wanted to reassure themselves that the film would be a colourful and comprehensible popular entertainment rather than a British period movie full of impenetrable cockney jargon. In a self-contained dream sequence, Ray Davies – playing the father of the young narrator and central character, Colin – is fantasising in a three-storey terrace house, as he performs his song "Quiet Life". Since the house has no front, we see the choreography of what's going on in every room, a sequence inspired by Jerry Lewis's *The Ladies Man*, itself a testament to the influence of the great Frank Tashlin on Lewis's directorial style and persona. Temple was introduced to Tashlin and Lewis by Richard Burridge, the writer and jazz aficionado behind the defining drafts of the screenplay, the ones which declared its core and its idiosyncrasies. Because it occupied such commercially uncertain territory – original film musicals were at this point still recovering from the box-office disaster of Francis Coppola's *One From the Heart* – there was frequent script tweaking during the extended prelude to principal photography, and other writers (Christopher Wicking, Don Macpherson, Terry Johnson) were intermittently brought in along the way.

Davies's wife in the scene (and the film) was played by Mandy Rice-Davies, whose notoriety in British history for her supporting role in the Profumo affair in the early 1960s was eclipsed for us by the fact that her hair caught fire during the shooting of our scene, a phenomenon none of us had ever witnessed before. And crucially, the long gestation period gave us plenty of time to cast. The young leads were identified early on. Patsy Kensit – who had appeared in Jack Clayton's version of *The Great Gatsby* aged six, and was now the 17 year-old singer in the band Eighth Wonder – would be Crepe Suzette, and the unknown Eddie O'Connell – a screen test hunch of Temple's – would play Colin. David Bowie and James Fox were the grown-ups, overlords of advertising and fashion respectively. At the same time, Bowie was also playing a goblin king in a very strange wig in *Labyrinth* for Jim Henson at Elstree Studios on the other side of London, which required some inventive scheduling, as did the massive task of building our own labyrinth of Soho streets and buildings at Shepperton under John Beard, whose first feature as production designer this was, although art directing *Brazil* a year earlier would have made him fearless. Each day, I wandered around the set in disbelieving wonderment before dropping by the production office, where I might encounter one producer emerging from a shower with a turban on his head and another updating the shooting schedule on a double Filofax, whose flaps opened up like a little doll's house.

16 days after the start of filming, my mother died. My travels to Scotland to see her – in hospital, at home, then again in hospital – had inevitably become more frequent during the months since her diagnosis, and I was ready for the eventual loss. I had been making this journey for some years, and had travelled there by plane, train, coach and car. In their different ways, they all took forever. When I finally arrived there, it always felt cold, even in the middle of summer, and local transport invariably appeared to be restricted in some way, through cancellation or delay, on the weekends I visited. It was as if all movement in the south-west of Scotland closed down at dusk on Friday evenings and re-opened in the grey light of Monday's dawn. It was a long

way from my parents' lives in south-western Spain, whose isolation had even less flexibility of movement, but had poetry and a pulse beat instead. In this part of Ayrshire, industry and poverty lay side by side – housing estates, sandstone tenements, half-hearted apartment blocks, identikit train stations, clocks at a standstill, sand dunes in the shadows of industrial plants. In compensation over the years, the young women seemed to have become more confident and stylish, the diet a little less congested with carbohydrates, the interiors less corroded by cigarette smoke, the contempt for culture less implanted. The sun sometimes brought colours to life, especially greens that appeared flattened under cloud cover. The country landscapes had a rolling symmetry that took one by surprise. Occasionally, a little church with a steeple would punctuate the far horizon like a cartoon.

My father organised a simple funeral, his serene sense of duty eclipsing his tremendous grief and loss, and he never let me see him cry. After the guests had left the cemetery on the hillside behind the town, we played a round of putting on the green which separated the house from the beach, and the next day took a walk together around Ardrossan harbour, the waters of the Firth of Clyde unusually still, and the islands of Ailsa Craig and Arran identified and discussed as they came into view. He had become an informed analyst of the area and could chronicle the ongoing history of every building we saw, pausing to raise his tweed cap in greeting to the passing ladies he knew.

When I returned to London, there were endless visits to Shepperton Studios – day and night, since the elaborately choreographed scenes which take place during the 1958 Notting Hill riots were labour-intensive night exteriors with large numbers of extras. Being an extra on *Absolute Beginners* appeared to be the summer job of choice for young Londoners. And not only was the film continuing to have budget difficulties, our fellow financiers Goldcrest were having their own corporate meltdown. Their historical epic *Revolution* had gone substantially over budget, and their cash resources and borrowing facilities were under considerable strain, with insufficient lines of credit to finance the films they were already committed to. Compounding this was their internal unrest. Sandy Lieberson resigned as head of production and converted his agreement with them to that of an independent producer. Then their chief executive James Lee resigned too, prompted by the lack of support from the board for him to be in charge of all production decisions. Then they were looking down the barrel of a very substantial write-off. And all this at a time when the average British person went to the cinema once every 15 months, the lowest rate in Western Europe.

Thankfully, the film's unswerving supporter and defender during its final stages of shooting was the star who made the most difference: David Bowie. *Absolute Beginners* finally completed filming, only to find itself instead in a vortex of immobilising post-production conflict as a succession of editors tried to locate and identify the optimum version of the film in the face of the escalating impatience and irritability of those who reviewed it repeatedly. There was, however, one all-eclipsing highlight that for about five minutes seemed to compensate for everything. As we drove up Wardour Street after discussing the film's lurch from crisis to crisis over dinner one night, Steve Woolley slipped a still primitive version of Bowie's title song into my car cassette player. I was overcome by its melodic beauty, its caressing warmth, its wistful and wilful optimism, and I felt absolutely certain that the song would be heard forever, even as the film might recede in the memory.

At that moment, I also knew Virgin would emerge from the unrest without regret.

CHAPTER FOURTEEN

The various projects that the time and money-consuming *Nineteen Eighty-Four* and *Absolute Beginners* had successively put on hold began to disentangle, rotate and reveal themselves like a slowly unrolling carpet.

Liberated from the noise and congestion of its predecessors, the soon-to-be-titled *Captive*, written and directed by Paul Mayersberg, quietly went into production as a lowish-budget film, developed by Virgin and financed as a UK/French co-production, with Irina (daughter of Peter) Brook and Oliver Reed in the leading roles. We had discussed making a series of similarly-scaled films with the producer Don Boyd – who had enabled me to research my Raymond Chandler book some years earlier – after remarking on how alongside studio pictures and arthouse movies ran another parallel track, one on which modestly budgeted but distinctive genre films of ideas and style such as Alan Rudolph's *Choose Me* and Alex Cox's *Repo Man* were attracting discriminating audiences, particularly in Europe. (Boyd's sometime business partner, the adventurous distributor Hamish McAlpine, had the unfortunate distinction of opening *Choose Me* in a couple of cinemas in Wales, where over its first weekend *no money at all* was taken at the box office. When asked if this had made him think twice about film distribution, McAlpine replied no, that all it had done was to reinforce his resolution never again to release a film in Wales.)

Filming began with several night shoots I attended at various locations in London, re-acquainting myself with how much more efficiently a crew worked when there weren't so many people around to deal with and be distracted by. Daytime interiors were comparably brisk yet thorough, and I was struck by Mayersberg's ease with the actors and crew, his intellectual acuity matched by his cheerful interaction. As part of its financing, the film was edited at Studio Billancourt in Paris, which I visited early one morning to find sometime Yes vocalist Jon Anderson in the cafe, rehearsing with fellow singers, amid tables congested with coffee and croissants, the harmony parts of a song they were all about to record in Billancourt's studio. It was like a scene from *The Umbrellas of Cherbourg*, one also prompting thoughts of the folkloric litany of Hollywood musicals, "let's do the show right here!".

For the score, I had earlier introduced Mayersberg to Scott Walker – whose album recording sessions with Brian Eno and Daniel Lanois had by then been abandoned – hoping they might strike up a musical rapport, but Mayersberg decided that he wanted to work with the composer Michael Berkeley, who in turn led to The Edge from U2 and his vocalist friend, the still little-known Sinead O'Connor. U2's own transformation from club band to stadium colossus was well under way, providing Virgin with soundtrack album protection that, as with *Absolute Beginners*, might compensate for possible film losses.

The Fringe Dwellers, which Bruce Beresford was about to begin shooting in Australia, involved a different financing approach from us. We didn't produce the film, but instead committed a guaranteed sum against international sales, one which would then be cashflowed by a bank until the film's completion and delivery. Beresford had earlier visited my office while in post-production on *King David*, the religious epic whose enduring highlight is Richard Gere's exuberant samba dance through Jerusalem in a loincloth, and with whose biblical setting his signature *American Gigolo* strut looks uneasily anachronistic. With a decade of popular Australian films behind him, and both best director and best film Oscar nominations for his first US picture, *Tender Mercies*, Beresford was on a roll, reflected by his confident and entertaining company. Picking up a copy of the novel *Absolute Beginners* from the corner of my desk, perhaps channelling his friend Barry Humphries's creation Les Patterson, he lapsed into a deadpan impression of a cartoon Aussie archetype of the period – "Colin MacInnes. Pillow biter, wasn't he?"

Then there was *Out of the Blue*. Although Mark Peploe had written scripts for the distinguished European directors Jacques Demy (*The Pied Piper*), Michelangelo Antonioni (*The Passenger*) and René Clément (*The Babysitter*), it was an ambitious call for us, on the back of a single BAFTA-nominated short film as a director, to explore as his first feature the prospect of an epic and expensive drama of wanderlust, collision and coincidence – the kind of thing Wim Wenders might have come up with, and later did with *Until the End of the World* – as his first feature. Compounding our folly, I encouraged Peploe and his co-producer Simon Bosanquet to go on a location survey to India and Egypt while he was in the middle of collaborating with Bernardo Bertolucci on a historical epic set in China called *The Last Emperor*, which a couple of years later ended up winning all nine Oscars for which it was nominated. In the end, it was impossible to set in motion a film like *Out of the Blue* without collectively focused attention over a sustained period of time. It never had this, and eventually our option expired.

Conversations about *Total Eclipse of the Heart* with Jim Steinman and Patricia Knop continued, the latter completing a first draft screenplay that went some way towards capturing the operatic irrationality of love that we were striving for, but it was difficult to think of a director who might convincingly bring it to life. I sent it to Alan Parker, with whom I collided occasionally and whose direction of *Fame* and *Pink Floyd – The Wall* had already shown a taste and skill for films grounded in popular music, one later reinforced by *The Commitments* and *Evita*. I thought we might take it to his friend and former colleague David Puttnam, who would soon be running Columbia, but Parker was in the middle of writing an adaptation of William Hjortsberg's novel *Falling Angel* with a view to directing it (as *Angel Heart*) when the script was completed, which is exactly what he did. His rejection letter came in the form of a very funny cartoon, another of his skills.

I had also spent some months trying, without success, to persuade Bob Rafelson to direct *Gothic* which, with a drug-addled seance in Switzerland at its centre, required someone who understood how to orchestrate escalating madness in a compelling way. I felt sure that the emotional intensity – first repressed, then unleashed – of Rafelson's three films with Jack Nicholson at this stage (*Five Easy Pieces*, *The King of Marvin Gardens*, *The Postman Always Rings Twice*) would give ours a combustible edge, and it helped too that, as an American outsider, he would bring a fresh, even anthropological, perspective to an account of intense young British dreamers going completely off the rails, and out of this feverish hysteria creating their own horror stories. Then one day, over lunch, I concluded that the right director for it was sitting across the table from me.

Although I had seen a number of his divisive films about misbehaving artists of various kinds, admired the stylish swagger he brought to them, and applauded his fearlessness in pushing extremes (Richard Chamberlain and Glenda Jackson, the latter rolling naked on the floor of a train sleeper compartment in the Tchaikovsky biopic *The Music Lovers,* comes to mind), I had resisted the idea of offering *Gothic* to Ken Russell, perhaps because the match was so obvious. It was two of his most recent movies, both American made, that most intrigued me and made me believe there was a conversation to be had. In *Altered States,* he managed to bring vitality to entire city blocks of Paddy Chayevsky's dialogue without allowing it to immobilise his film, and in *Crimes of Passion,* a kind of dark comic strip about a crisis in American manhood, he walked a tightrope of farce and horror with such deft assurance that one had no idea what was coming next. Somehow Russell also persuaded his *Crimes* leading actor Anthony Perkins – playing a deranged, amyl nitrate-sniffing evangelist preacher who stalks Kathleen Turner – to conduct his wedding to girlfriend Vivian on board the Queen Mary at Long Beach, after Perkins applied for an ordination licence from the Universal Life Church, one of those organisations that have historically proliferated in Southern California. This made Ken Russell almost certainly the only person in the world to have been married by Norman Bates from *Psycho.* By the end of our meal, I was convinced that our director and subject were inseparable counterparts.

On the morning of my father's 80th birthday, he was rushed by ambulance to the same hospital in which my mother had died a few months earlier. He had an emergency operation on his bowel, then developed peritonitis, so remained hospitalised over the ensuing Christmas and New Year. I would take the night coach from Victoria after work on a Friday evening, arrive in Kilmarnock in Ayrshire at dawn on Saturday, sleep for a couple of hours in a motel room, then catch a local bus to the hospital for the start of visiting hours. For the most part, my sister Lesley and I alternated weekends, unless there was a perceived crisis, in which case one of us would try to drop everything and travel from London to a destination rarely less than eight hours away, whatever combination of transport we used. There was nobody else to visit him. He and our mother had lived a contentedly quiet life together, and we were aware of the impact that her absence would have contributed to first creating, then intensifying, his pain and isolation. When months later he left the hospital to return to his chilly high-ceilinged apartment, with gale force winds blowing in off the Firth of Clyde, we encouraged him to move a little closer to us so that we could visit him more easily and more frequently, but he resisted.

After a long post-production cycle of conflict that occasionally bordered on bloodshed – each cut of the film generating more disagreement than the one before – *Absolute Beginners* moved towards its premiere. Julien Temple felt the film he had for so long cherished and imagined was systematically being taken away from him by the various editors brought in by Goldcrest, who in turn felt they were simply exercising their rights as investor and completion guarantor on a film which had considerably exceeded its budget and needed to be a commercial success if the company, after the expensive failure of *Revolution*, was to survive. I empathised with Temple, who had flown the film's flag for so long, eloquently declaring its ambition and its aesthetic – repeatedly invoking Minnelli and Donen and Tashlin and Fuller and the perfect aptness of the CinemaScope ratio – to whoever would listen. But the reality was that our script was too long, it took too long to shoot, the weather was against us in a way we might have anticipated better, and although we were remarkably successful at generating interest and anticipation – and employing most of the Soho population as extras during the shoot – it was infected at times by an undeniable vanity. Alluding to the high-style magazine of the time, *The Face,* someone who hadn't yet seen the film itself referred to something he called Absolute Beginners Syndrome: it was a film "made by, with and for the kind of person who'd read *The Face* from issue one". In other words, e*verybody* who thought themselves cool, and of the moment. We didn't set out to create problems for ourselves so that the movie would be more interesting to read about, but we did nevertheless. Much of the attention we received was attention we didn't particularly want but by then couldn't do anything about.

The press show preceded the premiere by a few days, and the reviews, given enormous prominence, were printed what appeared to be seconds later. One could immediately feel the resentment towards the perceived marketing hype, much of which had been self-combusting. Two rival newspapers – *Daily Mirror* and *Daily Express* – both headlined their reviews ABSOLUTE DISASTER. The *Evening Standard* confined itself to ABSOLUTELY ALL OVER THE PLACE. The type seemed so large that it may as well have been neon-lit for added impact. It was as if the entire future of the British film industry were dependent on *Absolute Beginners* – and that the film's primary obligation was to save Goldcrest from financial ruin. After all this, the premiere itself seemed like a gentle night out, although not unexpectedly it was also a well-dressed and over-populated one. I sat directly behind Princess Anne and wondered what kind of royal punishment might result if I took a piece of fluff out of her hair without permission. The film looked fantastic on the big Leicester Square Theatre screen, and the party afterwards was in a marquee erected in the square directly outside the cinema, making it the most perfectly located reception venue of all time.

A few weeks later, the film's US distributor Orion took the enlightened course of opening it in only four big city cinemas – including the Cinerama Dome in Los Angeles and the Ziegfeld in New York – to determine how widely it might play, resulting in a $21,000 per screen average and terrific reviews everywhere it played. Michael Wilmington in the *LA Times* wrote: "One of the most entertaining movies this year, and one of the few that shows real invention and audacity, along with big-studio technical flash. This is a picture that could be the first great movie musical of the 80s; it may carry the same meaning for our time that *Top Hat, Meet Me in St Louis, On the Town* or *A Hard Day's Night* held for theirs." So, in contrast to the UK's divisive saturation attention, the film was presented in the US as a kind of classy, special-event, big-city, pop-culture entertainment – perhaps its true destiny – and the following month was screened out of competition in Cannes.

Cannes 1986 was unusually and seductively quiet. There had recently been US air strikes on Libya, whose leader Colonel Gaddafi was himself targeted, and there was a rumour that in retaliation Gaddafi would bring his troops across the Mediterranean and invade southern Europe. Nowhere in particular had been identified in this piece of speculation but show business narcissism ran so deep that nobody could think of a more inviting or attention-rewarding war site than the Cannes Film Festival. So American movie companies in general – and the studios in particular – chose not to send their top executives to this edition of the festival on the grounds, one supposes, that the lives of those lower down the corporate ladder were worth less. The consequence of this drop in the population – and the fact that the absent individuals were people who tended to occupy more than their share of space – was that it was easier to access screenings, find tables in all the best restaurants, and take a leisurely walk along an uncrowded seafront to business appointments in offices and hotels at any time of the day or night. At the end of the bay, in perfect playful symmetry, was the galleon from Roman Polanski's *Pirates*, the opening night film.

Gothic was due to begin shooting immediately after the festival, so we invited Ken Russell to join us there. International distributors were expressing interest in the film, and his presence would help to increase it. As a measure of how prolific and successful he had been, he was the only director in history to have three first-run films (*The Music Lovers, The Devils, The Boyfriend*) playing in Central London cinemas at the same time. There was also the appeal of the cast (Gabriel Byrne as Byron, Julian Sands as Shelley, Natasha Richardson, whose mother Vanessa Redgrave was directed by Russell in *The Devils*, as Mary Shelley), the attraction of an innately cinematic script in an identifiable genre, and the fact that this was Russell's first British film for a decade. To my surprise, he had never been to Cannes before, despite a 25-year career of some distinction, and his 1974 film *Mahler* playing in competition at the festival – an absence he ascribed to being advised by one of the film's producers, David Puttnam, that his presence would not be required. The reality was that Russell could cause a stir there just by showing up. At a press conference on a sunny morning at the Majestic Beach to announce the imminence of *Gothic*, he arrived in pink shirt and trousers, red socks below them, snow-white hair blowing in the breeze above them, a walking photo opportunity who could also talk with a flourish. The following night, I escorted him to a dinner the festival held for Claude Lelouch, the director of *A Man and a Woman*, to which he had now made a sequel 20 years later called, inevitably, *A Man and a Woman – Twenty Years Later*. Russell and

Lelouch were seated next to each other and introduced, but the gulf in language, artistic taste and worldview became increasingly evident and their conversation tapered off after the first course, never to be reignited.

Such gatherings can work more effectively outside of festivals if the directors present are there to acknowledge a single venerable filmmaker they are all united in admiring. Virgin, which distributed Akira Kurosawa's *Ran* in the UK, had some weeks earlier held a dinner with the British Film Institute in London at which Prince Charles presented the great Japanese director with a BFI Fellowship, an occasion attended by the likes of David Lean, Richard Attenborough, John Boorman, John Schlesinger, Richard Lester and Hugh Hudson. The remarkable Serge Silberman – a veteran auteur-driven European independent producer in the tradition of Anatole Dauman, Alberto Grimaldi and Carlo Ponti – was said to have financed *Ran* himself from the profit made by his previous production *Diva*, the debut movie of a young Jean-Jacques Beineix. Kurosawa was by then 75, and *Ran*, the costliest Japanese film to date at that time, was considered to be the climax and crowning glory of his career (in reality, three lesser films followed before his death). Everybody showed up to pay tribute, and rightly so.

Back to Cannes. Although it was a little low on Americans, there was a tidal wave of Australians to compensate. The now completed *The Fringe Dwellers* was playing in competition, and while its director Bruce Beresford was unable to attend the festival, everyone else connected with the production did. Actresses Justine Saunders and Kristina Nehm were there, as was producer Sue Milliken, whom I accompanied to the print rehearsal that took place in the Palais des Festivals in the middle of the night, a prelude to the press screening and conference held the next morning, with the official festival screening following later in the day. This was my first experience of sleep-deprived, dream-state viewing – of watching a film practically alone in a giant 2300-seater ghost town under a roof – and it would not be my last. The Australian party was very hospitable – lunch in a private dining room at the Gray d'Albion hotel, a party at the Maschou Beach, and another at the Australian Film Commission office, with its coveted seafront balcony, after the official screening. I had several long conversations with Phillip Adams and Kim Williams, who ran the Australian Film Commission – charming, educated and articulate men I did not yet realise I would meet again quite soon.

At some point during each Cannes, I would have a meal with Pierre Rissient. Sometimes joined by mutual friend Todd McCarthy – who later made a film about him – we free associated film memories and made labyrinthine connections between them, like improvising jazz musicians in no hurry to relocate the main melody. His army nickname was Pee Wee, which caused some silent amusement. His first exposure to films was in a French village, mine in a Spanish one, and we shared that wonderment of movies coming to life at an early age in remote places where other entertainment was absent. He seemed to carry the whole history of cinema around in his head, and made me feel I did too when we first waded through the filmographies of Howard Hawks and Raoul Walsh. We both had a strong feeling for Fritz Lang's two-part Indian epic (*The Tiger of Eschnapur* and *The Indian Tomb*) and for Otto Preminger's *Whirlpool*, films even other cinephiles didn't talk about much. He made connections – between directors, actors, studios, decades – with a particular fascination with blacklisted filmmakers (Losey, Dassin, Berry, Polonsky) and had an appetite for gay conspiracy theories, some of them prompting disbelieving mirth at their improbability. In his pantheon of Hollywood's closeted homosexuals, Burt Lancaster and Tony Curtis on *Trapeze* were much more absorbed with each other than with Gina Lollobrigida, which is what, we extrapolated, must have subsequently ignited their remarkable performances in *Sweet Smell of Success*. Then there was the story about Montgomery Clift and O.E. Hasse – the actor playing the role of the murderer whose confessional secret priest Clift must keep in *I Confess* – taking their collusion one step further after hours. John Wayne and John Ford were also mentioned (although thankfully not with each other), and he would reach an absurd, defiant climax when he tried to persuade us that the *uber* macho Rod Taylor was really bisexual. And, of course, the size of certain actors' penises – Milton Berle, John Ireland and Steve Cochran all had garden hoses as thick as fire hydrants, according to Pierre.

His stories about being John Ford's press agent during Ford's late-career drunken visit to Paris were priceless, and his account of escorting a by-then practically blind Fritz Lang to see *Deep Throat* on Hollywood Boulevard a poignant absurdist farce. Many tried without success to summarise the elusive mix of elements that Rissient brought to what he did, whatever it was. Peter Debruge of *Variety* once described him as "at once ubiquitous and invisible", but it was director Claude Chabrol who provided the deadpan final word on the subject: "No one can tell you what he does".

When the festival finished, I went to Cumbria for the first few days of the *Gothic* shoot. Russell and his wife Vivian had evidently survived having Norman Bates conduct their wedding, and were living in the Lake District. When we began discussing possible locations, Russell knew exactly where to film the Swiss-set exteriors – just along the road from his house. What he hadn't anticipated was the wind. There is a morning-after scene at the end of the film in which the five survivors of a long and troubled night are having breakfast outside, trying to make sense of what has happened. In this idyllic setting, there was a gale so fierce blowing off the lake that the food on the table had to be secured to prevent it from flying into the water. A memorable on-set shout from the director – "nail down the Swiss rolls!" – was duly recorded. The following week we moved to the Palladian mansion Wrotham Park in Hertfordshire and remained there for the rest of filming.

He was the first director I had met who could have done anybody's job on a film except acting. He could look at anything and know exactly what adjustments to make, including none. He was the complete filmmaker, and perfect for this particular movie, in which the starting pistol goes off after the opium kicks in and things go a little crazy. He just had to calibrate that craziness in order to make the film effective, and he was an expert at that. The only problem for him was the composer we had taken on, Thomas Dolby. Russell knew a lot about classical music and you could tell he would rather we had gone to, say, Richard Rodney Bennett, who had scored his Harry Palmer film *Billion Dollar Brain* 20 years earlier. Dolby was a contemporary writer/performer/producer who played synthesiser and could therefore summon up a version of orchestral sound, so I saw him as someone able to bring musical literacy to conversations with Russell, while also giving a contemporary edge to the music itself. There was, of course, the recurring soundtrack album safety net factor for Virgin if the film didn't perform commercially. When we later applied for our Dolby licence, and Dolby permission to use their logo in our end titles, poster and paid advertising, they informed us that we couldn't because they were taking legal action against Thomas Dolby for usurping the Dolby name as his adopted professional surname. Even if Thomas Dolby wasn't *really* called Thomas Dolby, I asked, surely his popularity as a musician would be an asset to the Dolby Corporation? Evidently not. So, *Gothic* ended up as perhaps the only film in post-Dolby motion picture history to carry the truncated sound acknowledgement "in stereo", like some early test record for stereophonic sound with a sleeve photo of bespectacled middle-aged men in laboratory coats carrying clipboards.

An early invitation to close the London Film Festival at the end of November (with *Castaway* opening it) created exactly the right pressure on us to accelerate the completion of *Gothic*, and it was gratifying to see Ken Russell and Nicolas Roeg referred to as "two of the country's greatest directors" – as they manifestly were – in the festival's *Hollywood Reporter* announcement story. But other things were not going well. There were escalating differences of opinion and approach with my colleague Robert Devereux – then married to Richard Branson's sister, Vanessa – and annoyance at his peremptory manner and air of imperiousness. A long relationship with the producer Clare Downs, which had begun soon after my separation from Yoli, was also deteriorating perceptibly and accelerating towards an inevitable conclusion, its final hours spent on a dance floor at the Acropolis disco in Lindos on the Greek island of Rhodes, where she was making the film *High Season*. My dance partner was the actress Jacqueline Bisset, hers Alexander Godunov, a dancer of considerable fame and distinction, who had defected from the Bolshoi Ballet some years earlier and was now an actor who lived with Bisset. Bisset and I treated it like a frenetic workout. Godunov just hopped modestly from foot to foot with Clare. The irony was not lost on me. My taxi to the airport waited outside, motor and meter running. It was an aptly cinematic conclusion.

Back in London, a late-night preview of *Captive* – which those attending a paid session of *9½ Weeks* were encouraged to stay and watch – was a catastrophe. The gulf between my own perception of the film (ambitious, lush, tragic, dreamlike) and that of much of the audience (pretentious, absurd, worthy of abuse) was never greater. It was an English-language art movie, which would later play better in France with subtitles than it did in Britain without them. I completely believed in Paul Mayersberg – who after the Roeg scripts had more recently collaborated with Nagisa Oshima on the writing of *Merry Christmas, Mr. Lawrence* – and I felt for him and for what he was striving to achieve in the film, which, despite a handful of extended and thoughtful reviews amid the one-paragraph dismissals, simply came and went at only three London cinemas. Of those three, the exhibitor still managed to misinform us on the location of one of them, which was then wrongly listed on the film's limited advertising. It was a debilitating and demoralising experience, a long way from the childhood reveries of the little boy in Spain for whom films felt like a lifeline to the world, a gateway to a place of infinite possibilities.

There was little time to brood, since its producer Don Boyd quickly advanced his plans with *Aria,* a collaboration between RCA Video Productions and Virgin, in which ten directors would make ten short films, each budgeted at £50,000 and built around an aria selected from the RCA catalogue, one of them linked to a narrative device Boyd was working on that would punctuate the film. This being the time when MTV had invaded the cultural bloodstream and the pervasiveness of music videos made them almost a trading currency, it was quickly agreed that this was an inspired low-cost zeitgeist bullseye, navigating a pop aesthetic into a high-art field, an intoxicating combination at the crossroads of creative endeavour. This kind of talk dominated the conversation at a fancy media launch in New York, where RCA was based, with Robert Altman and Derek Jarman, who had already shot their segments, in attendance. Jean-Luc Godard had also filmed his, but while the remaining directors were later working on theirs, Godard decided he didn't like some of the filming he'd done, so reshot it at his own expense. Also committed were Bruce Beresford, Bill Bryden, Franc Roddam, Nicolas Roeg, Ken Russell, Charles Sturridge and Julien Temple. Some were opera lovers; others simply keen to rise to the occasion in good company.

Aria just got through the net. When I returned to London, there was a letter from Richard Branson informing us that the rumours were true: Virgin (excluding airline, holidays and clubs) was about to be floated as a public company, taken to the stockmarket to raise £60 million. As the subtext to this was clearly to attract investment by presenting as risk-averse a corporate structure as possible, I knew what this would mean to the film division – that we would no longer originate and bankroll movies as a production company but would instead pre-acquire distribution rights. Apart from enabling us to finance more films at less risk – which became my litany at each ensuing media interview – Virgin had bought a video distribution company (VCL) which operated all over the world, and it made sense to focus on feeding our own pipeline. Instead of gambling on a couple of bigger films a year – ones whose success was determined by a compound of unpredictable factors – we would also be taking a few steps up the recoupment waterfall, where our distribution guarantees, costs and commissions would invariably be paid before equity finance. What I tried to communicate to outsiders was that the change amounted to little more than at what stage we paid for a film, and that my supervisory interest in projects with which we became involved would remain pretty much as it was. But I knew that this would be difficult to realise, and that I would get little support from my now largely pragmatic group-think colleagues.

Back in the world of films we had financed and would soon complete, our friends at Atlantic – US distributors of *Nineteen Eighty-Four*, who had pre-bought *Gothic* – were anxious to see a cut. Mistaking them for predisposed allies, I sent them the best we had at that moment – a time-coded video of the fine cut, with no sound editing and a temp score, and a note emphasising this. My reward was their sudden withdrawal from the deal, silently and without warning. A few weeks later, we had Vestron on board instead, announced the day I arrived, unannounced, in Los Angeles, on my way to Sydney. Vestron, an exemplary distributor for the film, did well with *Gothic* in America – then went on to make three successive films with Ken Russell after it.

The reason I was on my way to Sydney was to visit Andrena Finlay, spend three weeks in her company and see where it took us. I had first encountered her at a party at the Chateau La Napoule, on the coast road west of Cannes, in May 1983 after the official Cannes screening of *Merry Christmas, Mr. Lawrence*. The film's star David Bowie, with whom I was yet to have dealings – these followed when we later met over *Nineteen Eighty-Four* (a score he didn't do) and *Absolute Beginners* (acting and singing he did do) – was sitting at the head of a long baronial table with only Jim Callahan, his minder on the *Serious Moonlight* world tour he was doing at the time, for company. Jim had been in charge of security on Mike Oldfield's 1979 European tour with the orchestra and choir, so I knew him quite well in the way people on the road do, which is really not that well at all – but

192

memory creates its own intimacy. So I greeted Jim and then I greeted Bowie, and nearby standing against a pillar on her own was Andrena, to whom I was introduced by Goldcrest's sales agent Bill Gavin, who appeared out of nowhere and whose date I assumed she was. We talked a little, and I was, well, *struck*. I remembered I had once seen her fleetingly across the bar at BAFTA in London, after her short film *The Privilege* had won a BAFTA and Virgin's first investment *A Shocking Accident* had won an Oscar within three weeks of each other, but she was surrounded by friends, and I wasn't one for glad-handing strangers in crowded places.

Fast forward to May 1986, when we met again in Cannes. Milanka Comfort – whom I'd known when we both worked at Virgin Records in London years earlier – came bounding across the Majestic Bar to greet me. She had been living in Australia and working in films since then, and behind her was her friend from Australia whose recent TV movie *Handle with Care* she had production managed – Andrena. This time we had dinner. Then another dinner in London. Then our respective relationships broke up, unknown to each other. Then I decided to visit her for Christmas. Then I did.

CHAPTER FIFTEEN

Travelling to Sydney via Los Angeles made the journey a little longer but significantly more agreeable. In the prelude to Christmas, the California light had a balmy serenity, the air unusually clean and cool, the mood gently festive. Although Virgin Films was now primarily a distribution company – in becoming so, losing some of the creative lustre associated with actually making films – three years of travelling to the US as a producer and potential financier meant I had by then had dealings with most people in both studio and independent circles, and could rely on relatively simple access to those with whom I hadn't.

At a time of year when executives were winding down and a project pitch didn't feel like an entrapment, this interlude gave me what I anticipated might be the final opportunity to present *Total Eclipse of the Heart* to studios on whose financing it was now completely reliant, and to make personal visits to Cinetel – who would soon be releasing *Captive* in the US more effectively than Virgin itself had done in the UK – and to our new friends at Vestron, who had enthusiastically acquired *Gothic* in the immediate slipstream of Atlantic's withdrawal. While the mood was benign wherever I went, I could feel that *Total Eclipse* was slowly evaporating, and I had little to report to the writer Patricia Knop during our otherwise affable encounters. There was a kind of placid neutrality in the air, compounded by the fact that I was just passing through. The recent release and remarkable success of *Crocodile Dundee,* already the second-highest grossing film of that year in the US, had changed the perception of Australia. Where I was travelling to next prompted much greater curiosity and speculation than where I'd come from.

So, for a few days I met people and did Hollywood things. I played tennis with Virgin's lawyer on the courts across the road from the Fox lot. I met up with old friends like Devo manager Bill Gerber, who had recently become a production executive at Warner, and Ken Russell's agent Peter Rawley, an erudite British expatriate who introduced me to interesting people. I spent an idyllic Saturday afternoon lying in the sun on a hillside in Topanga Canyon, listening to spellbinding stories about young actors of the 50s and 60s (Dennis Hopper, Dean Stockwell, Russ Tamblyn), close friends who all settled in that most remote of Los Angeles canyons to live the hippy rural idyll that was then flourishing – followed by a leisurely Sunday in the hills above Sunset Boulevard with Julien Temple, decamped there to lick his wounds after *Absolute Beginners* and preparing to direct his first Hollywood movie, *Earth Girls Are Easy* (aliens land spaceship in San Fernando Valley swimming pool, high jinks ensue), which would begin filming a few months later.

Although Hollywood had been in a constant state of mutation throughout its long history as the epicentre of filmmaking, its instability had increased after the purchase and absorption of United Artists by MGM in 1981, following the *Heaven's Gate* debacle and downfall. By now these corporate shifts had been compounded by a kind of historical amnesia and, although the scaled-down UA was at that moment housed in its own separate offices in Beverly Hills, it was populated by young employees who had no idea of the mighty artistic and commercial force it had once been. As I waited in its lobby for my meeting, a young messenger and receptionist were discussing "some old guy" whose name they were unsure of, who sometimes occupied an office along the corridor. The old guy turned out to be Billy Wilder, a director who had helped to define postwar Hollywood, and whose films *Some Like It Hot, The Apartment* and others were synonymous with the start of UA's glorious final chapter as an independent.

On my last day there, before flying across the Pacific for the first time, a sense of history prevailed again. I was invited to the Virgin Records Christmas party. Their office was a building which, seven years later, I would visit regularly when it became the headquarters of Gramercy Pictures, the American distributor of a film I was to produce. It was a convivial setting, and although I no longer worked for Virgin Records – while remaining a nominal director of it – it had been a very successful year for them, fundamental to which was their first US number 1 single – Cutting Crew's "(I Just) Died In Your Arms", a song completely unavoidable on American radio that week. Sometimes you can be present at such a gathering and witness a sight so improbable and so unique – a freeze-frame moment unlikely ever to be captured again – that it becomes indelible. Across the room, a cheerful and amicable encounter between Roy Orbison, the crown prince of emotional rock ballads for over two decades, and the former Johnny Rotten, now an American resident, who when still locked into his late 70s punk-anti-Christ persona would likely have been dismissive towards Orbison. And there they were, clearly enjoying each other's company and, in the banality favoured by show business caption writers of the period, sharing a joke.

There may have been direct flights from Los Angeles to Sydney at the time, but I wasn't on one. Mine – as always on this route, flying backwards in time, then crossing the international dateline and going abruptly forwards – landed in Tahiti in the middle of the night. As the passengers stumbled across the landing strip in a blanket of warm fragrant night air, it was evident that much of Papeete airport had closed down for the night, and that a solitary passport control functionary was minding the store, but for the presence of a ukulele player and hula dancer, who began their performance to these hallucinating sleepwalkers the moment the first of us entered the airport building and finished it five seconds after the last had moved through to the transit lounge. It was easy to imagine our entertainers back in bed and sleeping soundly by the time the second leg of our flight took off.

There was a beguiling lustre over Sydney in the early morning as we descended. Andrena met me at the airport. She too had a beguiling lustre, although a delirious traveller is rarely a reliable judge of this. Crossing all of Australia by train on the Indian Pacific – an idea we had once considered, along with trips to the Red Centre and the Great Barrier Reef – had evidently been dismissed by this stage, since the subject was never raised again. Instead, the prospective calendar appeared to be full of social engagements, particularly ones involving family and friends over Christmas.

It was a glorious time. We moved in together after the wedding reception of one of her school friends, and for three weeks hardly spent a moment apart. When the Christmas sunshine faded and the New Year weather briefly turned harsh, we drove south to Kangaroo Valley in search of the sun, and when we couldn't find it, flew north to Noosa in Queensland, where we knew we would. I watched the Australia-England test matches on television as Andrena slept off her afternoon swims in the motel pool. I was completely intoxicated with her.

At the crossroads of 1986 and 1987, its bicentennial still a year away, Australia was at the peak of its prosperity and self-confidence, a contented and optimistic country blowing a warm and welcoming wind on new arrivals. House prices were escalating, sporting glories (Alan Bond's America's Cup win, Jeff Fenech's triumph in the boxing ring, Pat Cash's singles victory at Wimbledon) celebrated, the international triumph of *Crocodile Dundee* stratospheric, the publication of Robert Hughes's *The Fatal Shore* an undeniable literary milestone, then-lawyer Malcolm Turnbull's humiliation of the British government at the *Spycatcher* book trial a gloating triumph. And everybody seemed to be having lunch, enjoying the spoils of their accomplishments under the most potent partnership of prime minister (Bob Hawke) and treasurer (Paul Keating) anywhere in the world at that moment. It was difficult to leave a city where you could still park directly outside the international departure area and linger uninterruptedly over goodbye kisses.

Six days after returning to London, I found myself travelling a third of the way back to Australia. The Delhi Film Festival had selected *Gothic* for its programme, and since Ken Russell was unable to attend, the producers were invited instead. The frequency, length and air conditioning of my flights were evidently depleting me. By the time we arrived in India, landing only on second attempt, I was already staggering under a corrosive wave of flu symptoms. Between encounters with stray cows roaming the streets and the confronting poverty of the city's more crowded areas, I fabricated enough energy to function at screenings, press conferences and meals, then retired to my bed at the hotel and wrote delirious telexes to Andrena. A day trip by coach to the Taj Mahal in Agra with a few other festival guests faded in and out of focus, but the building itself was extraordinary, the view across the plain from it spellbinding, the return journey endless. In a darkness intensified by my rising temperature, I was sitting directly behind Karen Black, an actress whose arresting, slightly cross-eyed gaze in *Five Easy Pieces* sixteen years earlier I had never forgotten. When she turned around to talk to me, her eyes were fleetingly strobed in the headlights of passing cars on the dark road we were travelling along, giving her a sudden ghostly glimmer. It was a sight as compellingly hallucinatory as I subsequently had watching *Gothic* alone, sick, on a balcony overlooking the crowded stalls of the cinema where films were shown after their official festival screening, wondering what impact watching a deranged Byron and Shelley invoking ghosts on screen was having on the largely silent, uncomprehending audience in turbans and saris, and what they might be making of the appalling on-screen behaviour.

While it was certainly no hardship to have dinner and discuss marketing plans with Oliver Stone, whose film *Salvador* Virgin distributed in the UK, or Carlos Saura, whom I surprised with my crude Andaluz village-boy Spanish when he visited London to promote *Carmen* and *El Amor Brujo,* I could never quite persuade myself that it could be as satisfying as producing their movies. Ironically for a company no longer producing them, we had two films – *Gothic* and *Captive* – scheduled for theatrical release in successive weeks in the US.

Andrena arrived from Sydney, established an affectionate rapport with my son and daughter over lunch an hour after landing, and continued the journey with me to the American Film Market in Los Angeles, which was ruled by improbably titled exploitation movies with corresponding poster art (*Assault of the Killer Bimbos, Demented Death Farm Massacre*) and more upscale independent fare for grown-ups that one suspected would never be made. For me, there was also the unfinished business of trying to persuade TriStar and Lorimar – the only two remaining US producer-distributors who had not already declined *Total Eclipse of the Heart* – to finance it. Andrena was there to advance her own projects, and together we set up an industrious little base in our hotel room above the swimming pool, the sound of other people's splashing punctuating our calls.

One weekend we drove up the coast to the Santa Barbara Film Festival, at which Vestron had decided to preview *Gothic* a month before its American opening. While my personal highlight was a lobby sighting of our hotel's owner Fess Parker – the eponymous hero of the Davy Crockett films I had seen as a child – my professional one was that the audience reaction to our screening was quite extreme, reminding me of the response to *Blue Velvet* when I had seen it in a New York cinema a few months earlier – fascination, disgust, disbelief, laughter, incomprehension, a sense that they had never seen anything quite like it. The following day, Vestron's conviviality and enthusiasm confirmed that I was not alone in my perception.

Another separation: Andrena back to Sydney, me to London, where news awaited me that Virgin's final production *Aria* had been selected for competition at the Cannes Film Festival. At first, it was invited to play on the second Sunday evening, a prominent enough spot for a distinctive high-profile film seeking international distribution. Then, just before the festival's line-up was announced, the proposal changed. They would programme *Aria* on closing night itself, with the nonsensical concession, clearly intended to appease, that a jury screening would be scheduled in Paris before the festival's start, so that we would remain in competition. Closing night also carried with it several unavoidable liabilities: many critics and tastemakers had often left Cannes by then, and the distributor of the closing night film traditionally paid the costs of the festival's closing night dinner, a dinner we had no interest in attending since we were planning our own. My resistance to this folly, in which none of my colleagues would join me, was pointless. Cannes invariably brings out the supplicant in every filmmaker, and even the mighty Warner, our distributor in France, acquiesced. The longevity and abiding status of Cannes comes from not being like other festivals. It's a place where absurd pageantry intersects with lofty artistic ambition, run on a fragile fuel tank of self-esteem, the single biggest commodity one needs for resilient survival in such an environment.

Despite the fireworks display that *Aria* might have provided, and the presence of those directors who were able to attend, Cannes that year was a combative and wearying experience. There were more great exploitation titles, of course – on this occasion, *Space Sluts in the Slammer* and *Surf Nazis Must Die* – and more conversations about films that would never materialise, with absurd speculative casting suggestions for each role. There was also, inevitably, a wave of wealthy outsiders who wanted to be producers. (One, an oil tycoon with blocked funds in South America, was seeking "a relationship that's a two-way street" – as opposed to, one assumes, a relationship that's a narrow dirt track which leads over the side of a cliff.) He was interested in a Texan rites-of-passage opus about a 16-year-old cowboy ("from boy to man"), a 40-year-old woman ("from trapped to free") and a rugged Texan banker ("from macho to caring"); and, of course, plenty of the talk typical of the time about output deals, overhead deals, all the deals one can imagine. The word itself practically carried an electrical charge.

In this vortex of folly and delusion, I looked forward to an encounter with the American producer Ed Pressman on the Carlton Terrace. I had seen him occasionally when he was producing *Plenty* with Meryl Streep in London a couple of years earlier. He was an unusually quiet man for a film producer, and the fact that his first movies were the early works of Brian De Palma, Terrence Malick and Oliver Stone attested to his fine taste in filmmakers. Ed was now seated beneath a giant billboard for the Pressman production *Masters of the Universe*, in a configuration which positioned his producer credit ("produced by Edward R. Pressman") to rest exactly over his right shoulder as he spoke, as if it were an onscreen caption. It was an amusing touch – and, he assured me, an entirely unintended one. As for *Aria* – a film whose unarguable distinction was that it resembled nothing else that year – the closing night of the festival finally came, the awards ceremony preceded our world premiere, and we won no prize. Despite assurances that the jurors had all seen the film in advance, we would never really know if they had. What we did know with absolute certainty was the total cost of the festival dinner – although, in the blizzard of invoicing that followed, it is difficult to remember who counter-billed whom for how much.

Andrena arrived in London again. The pathological fear of loss I had experienced since early childhood, compounded by the targeted acts of sabotage I introduced to ensure I kept feeling it, meant I had already proposed marriage to her on the last visit, and when she vacillated, I playfully insisted she must counter-propose to me before we could take the subject any further. We had spent so little time together that her idiosyncrasies were only now beginning to reveal themselves. One of them was that she had no taste for or interest in wine, just as I was developing mine. When I introduced her to the Roux Brothers' pioneering restaurant, the Waterside Inn in Bray, and opened a bottle of Puligny Montrachet, one of the finest white wines in the world, she grimaced at first taste and ordered a Coca-Cola instead.

We took a brief holiday together in Los Angeles and stayed in the back garden of the Roosevelt Hotel, across the road from the Chinese theatre on Hollywood Boulevard, full of ghosts and legends, and within walking distance of many of our favourite places. One morning, I walked through the lobby to find it populated entirely by people who looked like silent movie stars. By lunchtime, they were occupying all the lobby pay phones, talking to their agents as others awaited their turn. Laurel and Hardy made their calls from adjoining phones, as if under contractual obligation to stay close together. Blake Edwards was shooting his film *Sunset* there because one of its key scenes had actually taken place at the Roosevelt Hotel, in whose ballroom the first Academy Awards presentation was held in 1929.

I drove over to see Chris Blackwell and Russell Schwartz at Island Pictures about *Crusoe*, for which Virgin was about to put up a million-dollar distribution guarantee for the world outside North America. I was impressed by Aidan Quinn, the actor playing Crusoe, and had earlier wanted him for *Out of the Blue*, and I admired the producer Andrew Braunsberg's ambitious work with Roman Polanski and Hal Ashby, and the great cinematographer Caleb Deschanel, whose second film as a director this was. What finally made the project irresistible was that the screenplay was an intriguingly unlikely collaboration between the writer of *The Wild Bunch* (Walon Green) and the distinguished British poet Christopher Logue. Something compelling would surely come of it. It didn't.

Andrena's marriage counter-proposal finally materialised – by the swimming pool one afternoon – so, naturally, we drove straight to an antique shop on Melrose Avenue and bought a beautiful old engagement ring to acknowledge the event. It was very romantic. Not long after, and a little less romantically, we parted again, taking long flights in opposite directions.

Another visit to my father. He looked so buoyant it was difficult to believe that a year earlier I had sat beside his ambulance bed on a return visit to the hospital where he had almost died once before, and it didn't appear he would last this journey either. Now he was back to walking five miles every day, his eyes sparkled as he spoke, and he retained a capacity for wonderment that enabled him to gaze at a then-contemporary toy like a Walkman as if it had just been delivered by spaceship. I still felt an engulfing sadness when I went to see him – the draughty apartment, the tiny meals, the unyieldingly grey skies, the corrosive rain – and it particularly distressed me to see him on his knees in a gale cutting the stems of flowers so that they wouldn't blow away from my mother's grave. I told him I was going to marry Andrena and live in Sydney. Having lived apart for most of our lives – I went to boarding schools and married young – this did not appear to trouble him, since he had never challenged my independence, even when he found it incomprehensible. In his gentle way, he simply asked me if she was nice.

I was not in good condition. The nature of my work had become more fragmented and less responsible, requiring me to focus my attention in numerous directions with declining satisfaction. I also felt I was putting most of the energy into the long-distance relationship – writing the letters, making the calls, generating the forward movement, manically creating a timetable for my move to Australia and subsequent wedding, which we initially decided would take place the week before Christmas at Palm Beach, Sydney's northernmost stretch of sand, at the end of a peninsula where you can't go any further without driving into the sea, aptly reflecting my state of mind. Andrena was preparing to start a new film, which prompted preoccupation, uncertainty and indecision. I was impatient, insistent, insufferable. There were moments when there were no doubts about anything, but these would pass and a silent withdrawal would follow. I was living in an unsteady world of shifting ground, bouncing from one hurdle to another as if optimism alone might eclipse all obstacles. Sleep was rarely a problem but staying awake sometimes was. A compound of running, swimming, massage and reflexology was papering over the cracks of my spiralling anxiety. When I began routinely cancelling meetings and meals, the twin fuelling stops of show business, I realised I needed to bring everything to a halt. So I did.

I flew to Sydney, lived with Andrena in a motel on the Bondi seafront for two weeks, went for long mid-winter walks along the Pacific shoreline, watched films, accumulated energy and restored myself. Soon after my return to London I wrote a resignation letter to Richard Branson. Apart from a brief estrangement following my departure from *Event*, it had been 13 years, three months and three days at Virgin – a comprehensive education in areas of popular culture I could not have experienced in as potent and wide-ranging a way, or with as much unbridled freedom, anywhere else. Above all, it had taught me – a prototype introvert-loner – how to communicate. Richard replied with a warm and funny note reminding me of a previous occasion when I had threatened to resign and he had started shooting at me with a water pistol he happened to have on his desk at the time, soaking me in the process. This is exactly the kind of moment I knew I would never experience – and would miss – with any future employer. Reflecting what by then felt like a lifetime of dealing with media, I issued my own press release the following day. I consulted no one in the company, and nobody questioned me about it.

Andrena was still vacillating. She was weary and confused after her filming, proposing to come to Europe for what would inevitably be a romantically loaded couple of weeks, but at the same time wanting an opportunity for us to explore the banalities of daily life together without pressure. It was evident that she needed sleep and solitude rather than travel and stimulation. She said she felt under pressure. I was under some myself, and this was increasing as my departure date approached – personal history to deal with, work to finish, preparations to make, logistics of moving countries to attend to, people to say goodbye to, all taking up as much time and energy as I had. My children Jason and Louise, in a remarkable loving gesture of selflessness that astonishes me to this day, put my happiness before their own and encouraged me to go ahead.

So, I decided. Since the woman I loved and wanted to marry lived in Australia, I would go there anyway, and begin another phase of my life. While still anticipating it would be with her, I needed to strip away the conditional element to maintain my own momentum. I sent an application form to the migration branch of the Australian High Commission in London, outlining my reasons for requesting rapid processing. The approval letter came through 10 days before the departure date of my flight. As a declaration of intent, and a strategic burning of bridges behind me, I had already despatched 22 tea chests and a car on a cargo boat to Sydney.

A month before I followed them there, there was a violent storm one night in London, with hurricane-force winds blowing over many trees in Hyde Park, through whose wreckage I wandered in disbelief the following morning. Three days later, there was a dramatic stock market collapse, which had everyone running for cover in a different way: a force of nature quickly compounded by the force of a capitalist catastrophe.

All that remained was to sign letters of resignation from the ten Virgin companies of which I was a director – including two I hadn't even heard of – and to organise a leaving party at the Roof Gardens, which my much loved and profoundly trusted assistant of some years, Mary Volk, who had witnessed everything during that time, set about orchestrating. Richard must have been particularly pleased to see me go – or very grateful for something past and unspecified – to let me take over his domain for four hours on a Thursday evening, with an unlimited guest list and a correspondingly unlimited bar bill. The Gardens occupied an aerial block above the Derry and Toms store on Kensington High Street, and had been landscaped to incorporate greenery, nooks and crannies, and wandering creatures even more exotic than the clientele itself. The invitation was to join me for "a tired and emotional" evening, paraphrasing *Private Eye* magazine's then-popular euphemism for "drunk". It was like a giant life canvas of everyone who had made a difference to me in the 17 years I had lived and worked in London. In the party's final stages, I saw the impresario Michael White, himself synonymous with glittering gatherings, drifting between conversations, with the benevolent air of someone could dispense a party validation simply by his presence.

Two days later, I was having dinner with my children at the airport. Inevitably, there were tears, but we reminded each other that they would soon be on their own flight to Sydney to be best man and bridesmaid at my wedding to Andrena, from whom I had not heard for several days. When I landed 24 hours later, I discovered why.

There were a couple of contributing factors, one circumstantial, the other philosophical. The first of these had prompted the mysterious silence preceding my departure. It turned out that

Michael Jackson was in town to perform several enormous concerts and that Andrena, with a show business writer friend, had visited Jackson's manager Frank DiLeo in his hotel suite one evening and had drunk Mr DiLeo's very expensive champagne until she was literally legless. She was indisposed for most of the following day, and for the day after that as I travelled, but had recovered sufficiently to make it out to the airport to greet me on arrival. The second was that in her delirium – it may even have been one of the catalysts for it – she had become a reluctant bride-to-be with a residual crisis of confidence about our wedding, which was to be held just under four weeks later. The invitations, it turned out, were still at the printers, which was where they might stay.

After a stabilising lunch on the beach at Watsons Bay – the quintessence of Sydney harbour hedonism at a time when the occasional diner might still swim ashore to their table – we spent the rest of the day and night in a hotel room in the city and blocked out the noise of anything but each other, emerging a little steadier and more reflective. Soon we had an apartment to move into, and after we did so our world calmed down. Aware of how little time we had actually spent together over a year of intense courtship – we frivolously counted nine-and-a-half weeks – I really adored this woman and felt sure I could make her happy. The invitations went out, the children flew in, and so did Andrena's ex-boyfriend and a colleague from London. On the eve of the wedding, a small, cheerfully low-key groom party dined together and went to see, inevitably, *The Princess Bride*.

The following afternoon – under a giant Moreton Bay fig tree and between thundery showers that stopped for exactly the length of our wedding ceremony – she really resembled one.

INDEX